NUMBER POWER™

A Cooperative Approach to Mathematics and Social Development

Grade 2, Volume 1: Grouping, Place Value, and Informal Computation

Laurel Robertson

Shaila Regan

Marji Freeman

Julie Wellington Contestable

DEVELOPMENTAL STUDIES CENTER

2000 Embarcadero, Suite 305

Oakland, CA 94606

This material is based upon work supported by the National
Science Foundation under Grant No. ESI-9150104.

Any opinions, findings, and conclusions, or recommendations
expressed in this material are those of the author(s) and do
not necessarily reflect the views of the National Science
Foundation.

Number Power™ was developed by the Cooperative Mathematics Project, a program of the Developmental Studies Center,
2000 Embarcadero, Suite 305, Oakland, California 94606.

Design: Don Taka
Illustrations: Duane Bibby
Cover Design: John Sullivan/Visual Stategies

ISBN 1-57621-198-3

Contents

Acknowledgments

Many people were involved in the development and production of *Number Power*. We are grateful for their time, valuable suggestions, and encouragement.

In particular, we wish to express our deep appreciation to the Stuart Foundations of San Francisco and to Ted Lobman, president, for their faith in and support of our program.

We extend our sincere thanks to the Walter S. Johnson Foundation and staff, who provided not only encouragement, but also a bridging grant at a critical time.

We also wish to thank the members of our Advisory Board, who contributed enormously to the development of the *Number Power* program:

Joan Akers, California State Department of Education

Carne Barnett, Far West Laboratory for Educational Research and Development

Neil Davidson, University of Maryland

Carol Langbort, San Francisco State University

Nell Noddings, Stanford University

Ruth Parker, Collaborative Learning Associates, Ferndale, Washington

Paul Trafton, University of Northern Iowa

Jean Stenmark, EQUALS, Lawrence Hall of Science, University of California, Berkeley

Julian Weissglass, University of California, Santa Barbara

Many teachers piloted lessons and units, allowed us in their classrooms to teach or to observe, and provided us with feedback that helped shape the format and content of the program. We particularly wish to acknowledge the following teachers and math specialists:

California

Alameda City Unified School District
Jane Baldi

Albany City Unified School District
Nancy Johnson
Violet Nicholas
Susie Ronfeldt

Berkeley Unified School District
Carolyn Adams
Mary Ough

Moreland Elementary School District
Terry Baker
Pat Brigham
Wanda Binford
Cristine Bryant
Carolyn Cassell
Shari Clare
Jan Frosberg
Vivian Karpel
Lew Osborn
Terry Pomposo
Linda Stumpf
Gaby Tennant

Oakland Unified School District
Mike Butzen
Roz Haberkern
Alicia Rivera
Kathy Selleck
Ted Sugarman
Sue Tierney

Redwood City Elementary School District
Kris Dalrymple
Lisa Erskine
Frances Nuss
Ann Marie Sulzbach

Ross Elementary School District
Allison Quoyeser

John Swett Unified School District
Kay Balandra
Louise Bevilaqua
Alice Dorman
Marilyn Griego
Anita Pister
Jackie Schlemmer
Carol Westrich

San Ramon Valley Unified School District
Cindy Collins
Cheryl Gonzales
Deneka Horaleck
Lincoln Olbrycht
Sally Powers
Sue Smith
Ruby Tellsworth

Stockton City Unified School District
Jan Holloway

Vallejo City Unified School District
Howard Banford

Canada

School District No. 39, Vancouver, British Columbia
Shirley Brunke
Pat Craig
Joan Crockett
Wayne Gatley
Liz Gautschi
Linda O'Reilly
Jan Renouf
Carrie Sleep

The staff at Addison-Wesley was an additional source of guidance for us. In particular, we wish to thank the following:

M. Patricia Brill, Editorial Director
Michael Kane, Managing Editor
Mali Apple, Project Editor
Barbara Atmore, Production Coordinator

Finally, we wish to thank the staff of the Developmental Studies Center, particularly the following people, for their support and invaluable contributions:

Eric Schaps, President
Anne Goddard, Publications Editor
Lynn Murphy, Publications Editor
Susan Frost, Production Editor
Caroline Arakelian, Copy Editor
Susan Urquhart-Brown, Curriculum Developer
Allan Ferguson, Computer Specialist
Patrick Kammermeyer, Computer Specialist
Joanne Slaboch, Director of Administration
Pam Herrera, Director of Administration
Dan Solomon, Director of Research
Carol Stone, Evaluator
Margaret Tauber, Evaluator
Duane Bibby, Illustrator
Stella McCloskey, Administrative Assistant
Denise Wood, Administrative Assistant

About the Authors

Laurel Robertson
Director

Dr. Robertson has been in education for more than twenty years as a classroom teacher, staff developer, mathematics consultant, and director of several educational programs. She is past president of the California Association for Cooperation in Education and is currently on the board of directors of the International Association for the Study of Cooperation in Education.

Shaila Regan
Curriculum
Developer

Ms. Regan has extensive experience as an elementary school mathematics specialist and classroom teacher. She has also been a mathematics consultant and staff developer for public and private schools throughout the United States, and is past president of the Alameda/Contra Costa Counties Mathematics Educators.

Marji Freeman
Curriculum
Developer

Ms. Freeman has more than fifteen years' experience as a middle-school mathematics teacher and mathematics consultant. In 1986, she received the Texas State Presidential Award in Mathematics Teaching. Ms. Freeman is an instructor for Marilyn Burns Education Associates, consultant to Cuisenaire Company of America, and author of *Creative Graphing* (Cuisenaire Company of America, 1986).

Julie Wellington Contestable
Curriculum
Developer

Ms. Contestable has more than fifteen years' experience as an elementary classroom teacher, mentor for Language Arts and Mathematics, and mathematics specialist. She has been a leader in district and county mathematics committees and in California School Improvement Program reviews. She is an officer of the Alameda/Contra Costa Counties Mathematics Educators.

Preface

This is an exciting time to be a mathematics teacher. Educators and the general public alike are calling for fundamental changes in the content and process of mathematics instruction. Recent national reports document the need for change, describe new goals for the field, and suggest new approaches to teaching and learning.

Number Power™ is designed to meet the call for curricula that models new instructional strategies and content. The focus of the program is to support and expand students' emerging number sense. The *Number Power* program consists of three multiweek units each for kindergarten through sixth grade, and is intended to supplement or replace existing curricula aimed at developing number concepts.

The *Number Power* units provide opportunities for all students to construct and expand their understanding of number over time as they engage in and reflect on experiences that help them make mathematical connections, employ mathematical tools, work with others to solve problems, and communicate about their thinking. The units are designed to be accessible to all students and to meet the needs of students with diverse backgrounds and experiences. Each unit fosters the development of several essential concepts and may include other areas of mathematics, such as measurement, geometry, and data analysis.

Number Power takes a holistic, developmental view of education and is designed to enhance students' social, as well as mathematical, development. Cooperative group work and ongoing discussion about group interaction help students understand the need to be fair, caring, and responsible, and develop the skills needed to work successfully with others.

Number Sense and Social Development

Number Power is based on the assumption that we learn about the world through everyday interaction with our environment and with others. Academic and social learning are integrated naturally, rather than developed in isolation from each other. Exploration, questioning, discussion, and reasoning are all part of this natural learning process that begins at birth.

With this assumption in mind, *Number Power* has been designed to support students' mathematical and social development in an integrated manner by actively engaging them in exploration and reasoning with others. Students in pairs and in groups investigate open-ended questions; use a wide variety of tools; develop problem-solving strategies; collect, organize, and analyze data; and record and communicate their thinking and results. Students' sense of number is fostered along with their understanding of what it means to be fair, caring, and responsible and their disposition and ability to act on these values.

Number Sense

A sound understanding of number is indispensible to making sense of the world. Documents such as *Curriculum and Evaluation Standards for School Mathematics* (National Council of Teachers of Mathematics, 1989) and *Reshaping School Mathematics* (Mathematical Sciences Education Board, 1990) make it clear that the development of students' number sense should be a primary goal of elementary school mathematics programs.

The focus of *Number Power* is to develop students' number sense. In particular, the program is designed to enhance students' understanding of number meaning and relationships, the relative magnitude of number, the effects and relative relationships of operations, and referents for quantities and measures. *Number Power* is also designed to enhance students' abilities to apply these concepts to everyday problems.

Students come to school with some understanding of the meaning of numbers, of how numbers relate to each other, and of how numbers can be used to describe quantities. *Number Power* extends this conceptual understanding by providing opportunities for students to explore and use numbers as they solve problems, discuss their thinking, and make connections between their experience and the underlying concepts.

This cycle of concrete experiences and reflection on these experiences also enhances students' sense of the relative magnitude of whole numbers, decimals, and fractions. Students begin to understand, for example, that 24 is two twelves, almost 25, about half of 50, small compared with 93, and large compared with 3. They also begin to develop "benchmarks"—recognizing, for example, that 0.8 is closer to 1.0 than to 0.5.

Number Power strives to deepen students' understanding of how operations affect numbers— how, for example, adding 4 to 24 results in a far smaller change in the number than does multiplying 24 by 4. Students have opportunities to develop their own algorithms and to begin to develop a sense of the effect of using a number as an operator on other numbers—understanding, for example, what happens when a number is multiplied by 0 or divided by 1.

Number Power involves students in experiences that help them relate numbers to the real world. As a result of experiences such as these, students begin to develop appropriate referents for numbers used in everyday life and to develop a range of possible quantities and measures for everyday situations. They begin to recognize, for example, that a dog would not weigh 800 pounds or that it is reasonable that a new car would cost about $15,000.

Number Power provides opportunities for students to apply their understanding of number to problems and to everyday situations. Students collect, organize, and interpret data, and develop their own informal ways to compute. Within a variety of problem-solving and real-life contexts—such as cooking, surveying class members about their pets, or making a quilt—students are encouraged to

- make estimates;
- decide when an estimate or an exact answer is appropriate;
- make sense of numbers and judge the reasonableness of solutions;
- use numbers to support an argument; and
- make decisions about the appropriate use of different computational methods—calculator, pencil and paper, or mental computation.

Social Development

Traditionally, schools have taken a major role in the socialization of students, helping them become responsible citizens. In recent decades, this role has taken a backseat to academic preparation, as students and schools have been judged almost entirely by their success in meeting narrow academic standards.

Today, however, the stresses of our rapidly changing world require schools to refocus attention on students' social development while continuing to support their academic development. In order to prepare students for the challenges of the next century, schools must help them

- be creative, thoughtful, and knowledgeable;
- develop a lifelong love of learning and the ability to pursue their own learning goals;
- be principled, responsible, and humane; and
- be able to work effectively with others to solve problems.

The recognition that social development and academic learning are integral to schooling and occur simultaneously is a cornerstone of *Number Power*. In each lesson, students have opportunities to explore and solve problems with others and to discuss and reflect on their group interaction. In the process, students are encouraged to balance their own needs with the needs of others, to recognize how their behavior affects others, to think about the underlying values that guide behavior, and to develop appropriate group skills. Reflection on their experience helps students construct their understanding of social and cultural norms, and leads to a deeper integration of positive social values in their lives.

Using Cooperative Group Work in Your Classroom

Cooperative group work benefits all students, both academically and socially. When students with different abilities, backgrounds, and perspectives explain their thinking and listen to the thinking of others, their reasoning and communication skills are fostered. Additionally, they are exposed to new ideas and strategies, learn to be supportive of and to value others, and become more positive about themselves as learners and more motivated to learn.

What Is the *Number Power* Approach?

The *Number Power* approach to cooperative group work includes some elements common to most cooperative learning methods: students work in heterogeneous pairs or groups as they pursue a common goal, are actively involved in their learning, and have ongoing opportunities to share ideas, discuss their thinking, and hear the thinking of others.

The *Number Power* approach differs from other cooperative learning methods in several respects, but especially in its focus on social development. Beyond addressing group skills, *Number Power* places particular emphasis on encouraging students to be responsible for their own learning and behavior, and on helping students construct their understanding of

- what it means to be fair, caring, and responsible;
- why these values are important; and
- how these values can be acted on in their daily lives.

Another difference is that the *Number Power* approach does not specify role assignments for group work. Instead, the lessons provide opportunities for students to decide such things as how they will divide the work or how they will record and report their findings. Learning how to make these decisions helps students become responsible group members. Many of the lessons include examples of questions that help students think about how they made these decisions and what they learned that would help them the next time they work together.

The *Number Power* approach does not recommend that student work be graded. The goal of the lessons is to support conceptual development. The lessons are designed to be learning experiences rather than experiences that expect student mastery and strive to encourage exploration, creativity, and intrinsic motivation. Concern about grades can greatly inhibit students' willingness to take risks and explore alternative strategies. *Number Power* lessons do, however, provide many opportunities for ongoing assessment of student understanding.

Throughout all aspects of the *Number Power* lessons, the asking of probing, open-ended questions is paramount to helping students construct their understanding. The questions suggested in the lessons seldom have a single right answer. Many are focused on helping students examine and rely on the authority of their own thinking. If students are used to answering recall questions or to giving an answer that they think the teacher wants, they may initially fail to understand the questions or meet them with silence or irrelevant answers. Their willingness to risk will increase as they understand that explaining their thinking and sharing many strategies and solutions is valued and important. Their ability to explain their thinking will increase with practice.

Many of the *Number Power* lessons suggest the use of some easily implemented cooperative learning strategies that provide opportunities for students to share their thinking. (For more information about cooperative strategies, Kagan's *Cooperative*

Learning is particularly informative. See Additional Reading, p. 167.)

1. *Turn to Your Partner.* Students turn to a person sitting next to them to discuss an issue or question.

2. *Heads Together.* Students in groups of four put their heads together to discuss an issue or question among themselves.

3. *Think, Pair, Share.* Students individually take a short period of time to think about a question or issue and then discuss their thoughts with a partner. The pair reports its thinking to another pair or to the class.

4. *Think, Pair, Write.* This structure is like "Think, Pair, Share," except the pairs write about their thinking after they have discussed their thoughts. This writing then might be shared with you, with another pair, or with the class.

5. *Group Brainstorming.* In this structure, each group needs someone to record ideas. Groups are given some time to come up with as many ideas as they can about a topic or a problem, and the recorder lists all ideas. Then groups are given time to analyze, synthesize, and prioritize their ideas.

The *Number Power* approach recognizes that a strong mathematics program will include a variety of instructional methods. The program, therefore, includes some direct instruction and individual work in addition to cooperative group work.

How Are *Number Power* Lessons Structured?

Number Power lessons are structured to provide frequent opportunities for students to interact with each other and with the teacher. Group work and class discussion alternate throughout the lessons. Many lessons begin with a class discussion about such things as the goals of the lesson and how they fit with previous work, the mathematical and social emphases of the lesson, and the problem or activity. During group work, students are asked open-ended questions to extend their thinking, to help them

solve problems, or to informally assess their concept development. At times, the class meets to discuss strategies and solutions, and often new questions. The lesson concludes with an opportunity for groups and the class to reflect on their mathematical work and social interaction.

How Do I Begin?

Whether or not you have used cooperative learning strategies before, it is a good idea to start slowly. Begin with pairs rather than larger group sizes. Try some of the strategies suggested in the previous section. These and other strategies can be used as part of the teaching and learning experience in any subject and can be used to structure student interaction before, during, and after traditional or cooperative lessons.

An important factor in helping students become responsible, independent, and cooperative learners is the establishment of an environment that supports cooperation. A supportive environment makes students feel safe, values and respects their efforts and opinions, and provides them with many opportunities to make choices and decisions. The role you play and what you model are crucial to the development of this environment. For example, asking questions that help students solve a problem on their own encourages them to become responsible for their learning and shows that you value their ability to do so. Asking open-ended questions beginning with such words as what, why, or how helps students extend their understanding and become confident in their abilities. Likewise, asking for a variety of solutions to a problem and for explanations of how they were derived helps students understand that risk-taking is desirable, that you are not just looking for a "right" answer, and that you value their thinking. Also, encouraging students to respectfully ask each other questions about their strategies creates a safe environment for constructive disagreement.

The physical setup of the room is also an important factor. The arrangement should allow group members to have access to materials and to be able to communicate with each other easily. Sharing one desk or small table, or sitting at two desks side-by-side, is a good arrangement for a pair; a small table or a cluster of desks works well for a group of four.

Learning to cooperate is a developmental process and can be difficult for students, especially in the beginning. Students may, for example, have trouble balancing their own needs with those of others, taking responsibility for their work and behavior, or dealing with open-ended questions. Understanding that these difficulties are a valuable part of the learning process will help both you and your students be more comfortable.

Class Building

At the beginning of the year in particular, it is important to help students develop a sense of identity and community as a group in order to support and develop a sense of cooperation. Students need ongoing opportunities to learn about each other, to set norms for behavior, and to make decisions about their classroom. Activities such as developing a class name, logo, or handshake can lead to an "our classroom" feeling. (Many ideas for class-building activities can be found in such resources as Graves' *A Part to Play*, Mormon and Dishon's *Our Classroom*, Rhodes and McCabe's *The Nurturing Classroom*, and Gibbs and Allen's *Tribes*. See Additional Reading, p. 167.)

Class building is an ongoing process; the spirit of community needs to be developed and supported throughout the year. Class-building activities are particularly important after a long vacation, after you have been absent for an extended period of time, after illness has kept many students home, or when you have an influx of new students.

Forming Groups

Several decisions need to be made regarding group formation: the size of the groups, how to form them, and how long to keep them together. The *Number Power* program suggests a group size for each lesson, and that students be randomly assigned to groups that work together for an entire unit.

A major benefit of randomly assigning students to groups is that it gives several positive messages to students: there is no hidden agenda behind how you grouped students (such as choosing groups based on student achievement); every student is considered a valuable group member; and everyone is expected to learn to work with everyone

else. Randomly assigning students also results in heterogenous groups, important for cooperative group work, even though at times a group may be homogenous in some way; for example, all girls or all boys. The following are several ways to randomly group students. (Other suggestions can be found in the Johnsons' *Circle of Learning*. See Additional Reading, p. 167.)

1. Have students number off and have the ones form a group, the twos form a group, and so on.

2. Have students take a playing card or an ice cream stick with a number on it and find others with the same number.

3. Have students take a card with an equation or short word problem on it and form a group with others who have an equation or word problem with the same solution.

4. Cut magazine pictures into the same number of pieces as members in a group. Have students pick a piece and find others with pieces of the same puzzle.

Keeping groups together for an entire unit provides an opportunity for students to develop and expand their interpersonal skills and their understanding of group interaction. Students learn to work through and learn from problems, and to build on successful methods of interaction. Long-term group work also allows students to build on their mathematical discoveries.

Team Building

Each time new long-term groups are formed, it is important to provide opportunities for students to get better acquainted, to develop a sense of identity as a team, and to begin to develop their working relationship. Each *Number Power* unit begins with a team-building activity. (The references suggested under Class Building also are good sources for additional team-building activities.)

During team-building activities, helping students label, discuss, and analyze behavior lays a foundation for their future group work. Open-ended questions can draw students' attention to their interaction, to their behavior that helps the group, and to how they might solve problems that have arisen.

Such questions might, for example, encourage students to talk about how they worked together; what group skills they used; how they wish to treat each other; why it is important to be fair, caring, and responsible; what problems they had; and the ways they wish to work together the next time.

What Is My Role?

One of the main goals of cooperative group work is to encourage students to do their own thinking and to take responsibility for their own learning. Your role is vital to the process of students becoming independent and interdependent learners. In addition to setting the environment for cooperation, this role includes planning and introducing the lesson, facilitating group work, helping students reflect, and helping students say good-bye.

Planning

Reading a *Number Power* unit, Overview and lessons, prior to implementation will help you make decisions about how to connect the lessons with students' previous experiences, and about the social values and group skills that might be emphasized throughout the unit. The group skills listed on the first page of each lesson are suggestions based on the type of student interaction that might occur in that lesson. (Listening skills, for example, might be the focus of a lesson in which students are explaining their thinking to others.) However, the developmental level of your students, their previous cooperative group experiences, and level of cooperation they demonstrate may lead you to choose other skills as a focus. You might also wish to develop a theme for a unit, such as communicating with others.

The following list of questions may help you as you plan. The *Number Power* lessons incorporate suggestions for many of them.

- What are the important *mathematical concepts* of the lesson? How are they linked with previous work and long-term goals?
- What are some possible opportunities for supporting social, as well as mathematical, learning?
- Is the lesson *interesting, accessible,* and *challenging* for all students? What modifications are needed?

- What *room arrangement* will be best for the lesson?
- What *materials* will be needed for the lesson?
- How will time for *student discussion* and *work* be maximized?
- How will *interdependence* among group members be encouraged?
- How will the lesson provide opportunities for students to *make decisions* and *take responsibility* for their learning and behavior?
- What will you be looking for as you *observe* group work?
- What *open-ended questions* might extend students' thinking?
- How will *assessment* be linked with instruction?
- What are appropriate *extension activities* for groups that finish early or for the next day?

Introducing the Lesson

Many *Number Power* lessons begin with questions that ask students to reflect on previous lessons or experiences, or pose a problem for students to discuss. Such questions are often followed with discussion about a problem or investigation that students will undertake and about specific cooperative group skills that might help them work effectively.

Discussing group skills at the beginning of the lesson provides students with models for positive interaction and with language to discuss their interaction. Vary the way these group skills are discussed. You might choose, for example, to emphasize a skill such as listening to others, then have students discuss what it means to listen, how others will know that they are being listened to, how listening might help their group work, and how listening to others relates to the values of being fair, caring, and responsible. You might, instead, ask groups to discuss and choose skills that they think are important to the functioning of their group, or ask students to discuss what they have learned about working together that will help them in this new lesson. At other times, you could have students role-play the activity and then, as a class, discuss what they observed about the group interaction and what group skills they think might be particularly important to their work. For some lessons, you might choose not to discuss group interaction at all during the introduction. No matter how and when you choose to discuss the social emphases of the lesson and the group skills with students, it is important to remember that social understanding is constructed through many opportunities to work with others and reflect on their experience.

Facilitating Group Work

During group work, ask thoughtful, probing, open-ended questions. The focus of such questions is to help students define the problems they are investigating, to help them solve interpersonal problems, to help them take responsibility for their learning and behavior, and to extend and informally assess their thinking.

As students begin group work, observe each group to be sure that students have understood the task and have no insurmountable problems; then focus on a few groups and observe each of them long enough to see what is really happening. This will provide you with information about students' ability to work together, their involvement in the activity, and their mathematical and social understanding. Such observation will also give you ideas for questions you might ask, and help you determine what other experiences students may need.

At times during group work, you may decide to intervene to refocus a group, to help them see a problem from another perspective, to ask questions that extend mathematical and social learning, or to assess understanding. When you intervene to assess or extend thinking, try not to interrupt the flow of the group work. Wait for a natural pause in the action. Ask open-ended questions that require progressively more thought or understanding. (Each *Number Power* lesson suggests sample questions to probe students' thinking about number and number relationships, to help them think about how they are solving problems, and to help them analyze their group work.) If a group is having difficulty, allow members time to solve a problem themselves before you intervene. Then, ask key questions to help them resolve the difficulty, rather than solving the problem for them or giving lengthy explanations.

Helping Students Reflect

Reflection on the mathematical and social aspects of group work helps students develop their conceptual understanding, build on past learning experiences, and connect their experience to long-term learning goals. Questioning before, during, and after group work encourages students to consider such important issues as, "What does it mean to be responsible?" and "How did my behavior affect others in the group?" and extends their mathematical thinking. *Number Power* lessons incorporate several methods to structure ongoing reflection, including group discussion, writing, and whole-class discussions. Each *Number Power* unit ends with a transition lesson to provide students with an opportunity to reflect on their mathematical work and group interaction during the unit.

Helping Students Say Good-Bye

When it is time to disband groups that have been working together for some time, it is important to provide opportunities for students to express their feelings and to say good-bye. The transition lessons at the end of each *Number Power* unit are designed for this purpose. You may wish to do some other parting activities, such as:

1. *Group Memories Bulletin Board.* Have groups write favorite memories about their group work or about each other and then post them on a bulletin board labeled "Group Memories."

2. *Group Memory Books.* Have groups make a book that includes work from their favorite investigations, comments from each member about what they liked about the unit and working together with each other, and a picture or drawing of the group.

3. *Thank-You Letters.* Have group members write thank-you letters to each other expressing appreciation for something specific.

4. *Good-bye Celebrations.* Have each group plan a way to celebrate their work together.

(For ideas for parting or closing activities, see Rhodes and McCabe's *The Nurturing Classroom* and Gibbs and Allen's *Tribes.* See Additional Reading, p. 167.)

Number Power Format

The *Number Power* program for Grade 2 consists of three units of eight to ten lessons each. In Unit 1, students group and count, and explore number patterns. In Unit 2, students group by tens and hundreds, explore place value concepts, and compute informally. In Unit 3, students sort and classify, compute informally, and explore the relationships between operations. These experiences are designed to foster students' understanding of our number system and, over time, help students construct their understanding of the relative magnitude of numbers, place value concepts, the meaning and use of operations, and how operations relate to one another. The *Number Power* program also helps students develop their problem-solving abilities. Students are encouraged to formulate and test hypotheses, to build theories, and to evaluate problem-solving strategies.

The *Number Power* program for Grade 2 additionally fosters students' understanding of and commitment to the values of fairness, caring, and responsibility. The lessons help students develop group skills, such as the ability to share the work and to make decisions. Throughout the units, students are encouraged to take responsibility for their learning and behavior and to reflect on how their behavior affects the work, others in the group, and themselves.

Unit Format

Each unit includes an Overview, a class-building or team-building lesson, conceptual lessons, and a transition lesson.

Overview

The Overview will acquaint you with the unit and offer suggestions for implementation. This section provides a synopsis of all the lessons, a discussion of the major mathematical concepts and social understandings that the lessons help students develop, and a list of all the materials you will need for the unit. The Overview also includes a discussion of informal assessment techniques you might use throughout the unit, and a summary of the specific types of student writing opportunities in the unit.

Class-Building and Team-Building Lessons

Each unit begins with a team-building or class-building lesson to help group members become acquainted, to begin to develop their sense of unity as a group or as a class, and to develop their group skills. These lessons focus on developing students' understanding of why these skills are important for the effective functioning of their group. You may wish to do more than the one class-building or team-building lesson suggested. Other ideas can be found in *A Part to Play*, *Tribes*, *Our Classroom*, and *The Nurturing Classroom* (listed in Additional Reading, p. 167).

Interior Pages

Some lessons begin with a section titled Before the Lesson (I). This section suggests student activities or material preparation that you may need to undertake prior to the lesson.

The lesson is divided into three columns. The first column (J) provides notes and suggestions for you. In some lessons, this column also contains an assessment icon (K) accompanied by suggestions for informal assessment.

The second column (L) is the lesson plan itself and includes sample open-ended questions to probe and extend students' thinking.

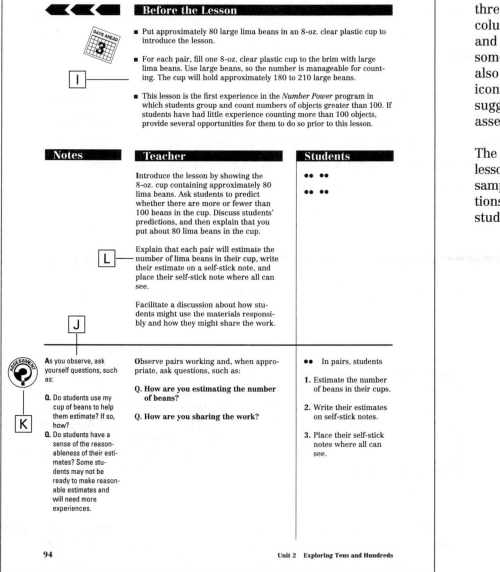

Before the Lesson

DAYS AHEAD 3

I

- Put approximately 80 large lima beans in an 8-oz. clear plastic cup to introduce the lesson.

- For each pair, fill one 8-oz. clear plastic cup to the brim with large lima beans. Use large beans, so the number is manageable for counting. The cup will hold approximately 180 to 210 large beans.

- This lesson is the first experience in the *Number Power* program in which students group and count numbers of objects greater than 100. If students have had little experience counting more than 100 objects, provide several opportunities for them to do so prior to this lesson.

Notes | Teacher | Students

Introduce the lesson by showing the 8-oz. cup containing approximately 80 lima beans. Ask students to predict whether there are more or fewer than 100 beans in the cup. Discuss students' predictions, and then explain that you put about 80 lima beans in the cup.

L — Explain that each pair will estimate the number of lima beans in their cup, write their estimate on a self-stick note, and place their self-stick note where all can see.

Facilitate a discussion about how students might use the materials responsibly and how they might share the work.

J

K — As you observe, ask yourself questions, such as:

Q. Do students use my cup of beans to help them estimate? If so, how?

Q. Do students have a sense of the reasonableness of their estimates? Some students may not be ready to make reasonable estimates and will need more experiences.

Observe pairs working and, when appropriate, ask questions, such as:

Q. How are you estimating the number of beans?

Q. How are you sharing the work?

•• In pairs, students

1. Estimate the number of beans in their cups.

2. Write their estimates on self-stick notes.

3. Place their self-stick notes where all can see.

94

Unit 2   Exploring Tens and Hundreds

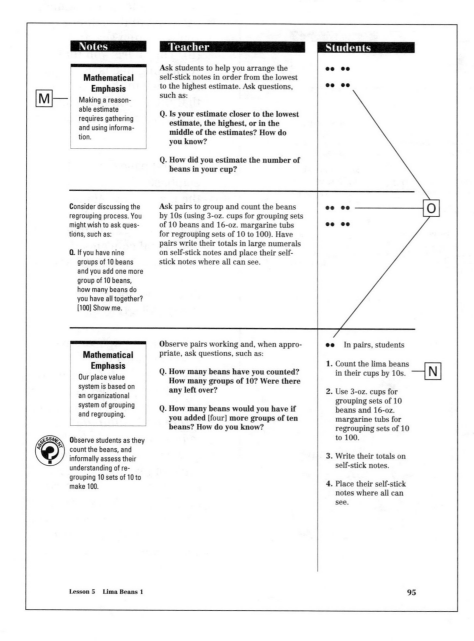

The boxes (M) suggest important mathematical and social concepts as the focus of your open-ended questions in that portion of the lesson.

The third column (N) describes the student work. It includes icons (O), described below, that indicate how the students are grouped for each section of the lesson.

Group Size Icons

Whole class icons

Teacher talks with the whole class, prior to grouping students, or after group work is complete.

Teacher talks with the whole class, already in groups of four.

Teacher talks with the whole class, already in pairs.

Student work icons

Students work in groups of four.

Students work in pairs.

Students work individually.

The content within the image:

Notes

M

Mathematical Emphasis
Making a reasonable estimate requires gathering and using information.

Consider discussing the regrouping process. You might wish to ask questions, such as:

Q. If you have nine groups of 10 beans and you add one more group of 10 beans, how many beans do you have all together? [100] Show me.

Mathematical Emphasis
Our place value system is based on an organizational system of grouping and regrouping.

ASSESSMENT

Observe students as they count the beans, and informally assess their understanding of regrouping 10 sets of 10 to make 100.

Teacher

Ask students to help you arrange the self-stick notes in order from the lowest to the highest estimate. Ask questions, such as:

Q. Is your estimate closer to the lowest estimate, the highest, or in the middle of the estimates? How do you know?

Q. How did you estimate the number of beans in your cup?

Ask pairs to group and count the beans by 10s (using 3-oz. cups for grouping sets of 10 beans and 16-oz. margarine tubs for regrouping sets of 10 to 100). Have pairs write their totals in large numerals on self-stick notes and place their self-stick notes where all can see.

Observe pairs working and, when appropriate, ask questions, such as:

Q. How many beans have you counted? How many groups of 10? Were there any left over?

Q. How many beans would you have if you added [four] more groups of ten beans? How do you know?

Students

O

N

In pairs, students

1. Count the lima beans in their cups by 10s.

2. Use 3-oz. cups for grouping sets of 10 beans and 16-oz. margarine tubs for regrouping sets of 10 to 100.

3. Write their totals on self-stick notes.

4. Place their self-stick notes where all can see.

Lesson 5   Lima Beans 1   95

Lesson Format

First Page The first page provides you with the logistical information you need for the lesson.

UNIT 2 Exploring Tens and Hundreds   **Lesson 5**

Lima Beans 1

A — Students use a referent to help them estimate the number of lima beans in a container. They then group and count the beans by hundreds, tens, and ones, and compare their estimate with the actual number.

B DAYS AHEAD **3**

C — **Mathematical Emphasis**
In this lesson, students
- Make an estimate.
- Group and count by 100s, 10s, and 1s.

Students add to their understanding that
E —
- Making a reasonable estimate requires gathering and using information.
- Our place value system is based on an organizational structure of grouping and regrouping.

Social Emphasis — **D**
In this lesson, students
- Share the work.
- Use materials responsibly.

Students continue to
- Develop appropriate group skills. — **F**
- Analyze the effect of behavior on others and on the group work.

Group Size: 2 — **H**

Teacher Materials
- 8-oz. cup with about 80 beans (see Before the Lesson)

Student Materials
Each pair needs
- 8-oz. cup filled with beans (see Before the Lesson)
- Twenty to thirty 3-oz. paper cups for grouping sets of 10 beans — **G**
- Two or three 16-oz. margarine tubs for grouping sets of 100 beans
- 2 self-stick notes
- Two-Hundred Chart (see Lesson 3)

Each student needs
- Folder (from Lesson 2)

Lesson 5   Lima Beans 1   93

Notice the lesson summary (A). Next to the summary you will often see an icon (B). This alerts you that something needs your attention prior to the lesson or that the lesson has a special focus: team building or transition.

The first page details the dual emphasis of the lesson. It lists the mathematical and social emphases (C and D), as well as the essential mathematical and social concepts the lesson helps develop (E and F). (See Planning, p. xiv, for a discussion about choosing group skills.)

On the first page you will also find a list of the materials specific to the lesson (G) and the suggested group size (H). *It is assumed that calculators and manipulative materials are available to students at all times for them to use at their discretion, and that the materials listed for students are available to groups in their work area at the start of the lesson, unless otherwise indicated in a lesson.*

Conceptual Lessons

The lessons that follow the team-building lessons focus on developing and extending students' sense of number through a variety of cooperative problem-solving experiences. Students use materials such as beans, peanuts, paper airplanes, and calculators to explore grouping and counting, place value, and operations. The lessons also provide opportunities for students to develop their abilities to work together effectively and to reflect on both their mathematical and social experience.

Transition Lessons

Each unit ends with a transition lesson that encourages students to reflect on their mathematical work throughout the unit and to make generalizations and connections. This lesson is also designed to encourage students to think about their group interaction, their successes and problems, and the things they have learned that will help them in future group work.

In addition to this reflection, the transition lesson allows students to express appreciation for each other and to celebrate their work together. After students have worked as a group for a period of time, it may be difficult for them to face separation and move to a new group; the transition lesson gives students a chance to make this break more easily by giving them time to acknowledge their attachment to their group and providing ways to say good-bye.

Last Page— Extensions

It seems to be a law of nature that cooperative groups seldom finish their work at the same time. To help manage this and to further students' conceptual development, two additional types of activities are included at the end of each lesson.

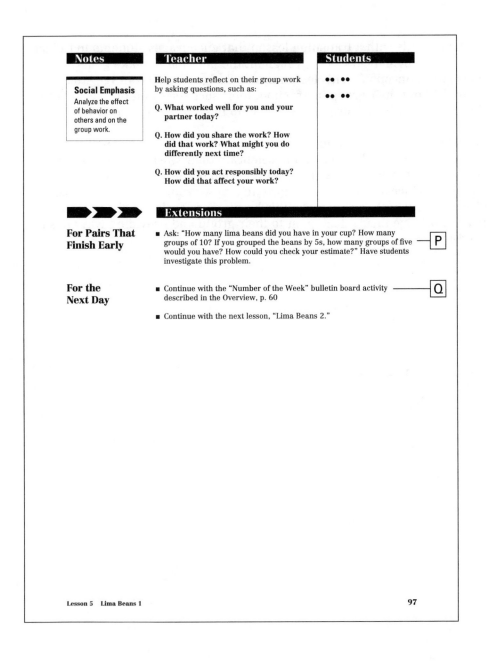

Notes	Teacher	Students
Social Emphasis Analyze the effect of behavior on others and on the group work.	Help students reflect on their group work by asking questions, such as: Q. What worked well for you and your partner today? Q. How did you share the work? How did that work? What might you do differently next time? Q. How did you act responsibly today? How did that affect your work?	•• •• •• ••

Extensions

For Pairs That Finish Early

■ Ask: "How many lima beans did you have in your cup? How many groups of 10? If you grouped the beans by 5s, how many groups of five would you have? How could you check your estimate?" Have students investigate this problem. — [P]

For the Next Day

■ Continue with the "Number of the Week" bulletin board activity described in the Overview, p. 60 — [Q]

■ Continue with the next lesson, "Lima Beans 2."

Lesson 5 Lima Beans 1   97

The first, "For Pairs [or Groups] That Finish Early" (P), suggests activities for groups to engage in as other groups complete their lesson work. The second, "For the Next Day" (Q), further develops concepts or gives students more experience with the same concepts before moving on to the next lesson in the unit. Some of the activities foster students' social, as well as academic, learning.

Grouping and Number Patterns

Mathematical Development

This unit provides students with many opportunities to count by various groupings, to explore number patterns, and to collect and analyze data. Students also use mental computation and calculators to compute. These experiences build on students' sense of whole numbers and help them construct their conceptual understanding of our number system. Experiences with grouping and counting by various group sizes are particularly important for students prior to more formal exploration of grouping by hundreds, tens, and ones.

Social Development

The social focus of this unit is to further develop students' group skills, particularly ways to share the work, to help each other, and to explain their thinking. Open-ended questions help students examine how the underlying values of fairness, caring, and responsibility relate to behavior and how their behavior affects their work and interaction. Students are encouraged to discuss and reflect on ways to work effectively and to solve problems.

Students are randomly assigned to pairs that stay together throughout the unit. In Lesson 5, pairs work together as groups of four.

Mathematical Emphasis

Conceptually, experiences in this unit help students construct their understanding that

- Quantities of objects and sets of data can be grouped and counted in various ways.

- Numbers can be used to describe quantities.

- Numbers can be composed and decomposed.

- Once a rule to generate a pattern has been identified, the pattern can usually be extended.

- The same pattern can occur in a variety of settings.

- Operations can be carried out in a variety of ways.

- Questions about our world can be asked, and data about those questions can be collected, organized, and analyzed.

Social Emphasis

Socially, experiences in this unit help students to

- Develop appropriate group skills.

- Analyze the effect of behavior on others and on the group work.

- Relate the values of fairness, caring, and responsibility to behavior.

Lessons

This unit includes ten lessons, plus an ongoing bulletin board activity. The calendar icon indicates that some preparation is needed or that an experience is suggested for students prior to that lesson.

1. How Many Groups?
(page 7)

Class-building lesson in which students explore how to divide the class into different-size groups.

2. Group It!
(page 11)

Ongoing grouping lesson in which pairs group and count objects in baggies, and record their results.

3. How Many Buttons?
(page 17)

Grouping lesson in which pairs predict the number of buttons in a handful and then count the buttons by various groupings.

4. More Buttons
(page 21)

Data analysis lesson in which pairs organize and analyze the data from the previous lesson.

5. Friendship Chain
(page 25)

Problem-solving lesson in which students determine the number of sheets of paper needed to make a class Friendship Chain and then make the chain.

6. Family Friendship Chain
(page 31)

Data analysis lesson in which pairs compute and graph the number of hands in their families, then discuss the data.

7. Count with Calculators
(page 35)

Calculator lesson in which pairs count by various groupings to reach a target number of 100.

8. Calculator Patterns
(page 41)

Calculator lesson in which pairs explore number patterns on calculators and Hundred Charts.

9. More Calculator Patterns
(page 47)

Calculator lesson in which pairs explore and compare number patterns.

10. Autograph Book
(page 53)

Transition lesson in which pairs reflect on their work together, count and group by 10s, compute informally, and make a thumbprint autograph book.

"Number of the Week" Bulletin Board

This ongoing activity provides opportunities for students to explore numbers. At the beginning of each week, post a numeral on the bulletin board—for example, 56. Ask pairs to write at least two factual statements about 56, such as "56 is about half of 100," "56 is the same as 50 plus 6," or "My grandfather is almost 56." Have pairs choose one of their statements, write it in large letters on a sentence strip, and post it on the bulletin board. At the end of the week, ask students to use their calculators to verify the statements. Ask questions, such as:

Q. Do you agree or disagree with this statement? Why?

Q. How would you rewrite this statement to make it true?

Q. What else could we say about this number?

Materials

The materials needed for the unit are listed below. The first page of each lesson lists the materials specific to that lesson. Blackline masters for transparencies and group record sheets are included at the end of each lesson. Transparencies and other materials are available in the *Number Power* Package for Grade 2.

Throughout the unit, you will need access to an overhead projector, and students will need access to supplies such as counters, calculators, scissors, crayons, rulers, glue sticks, paper, and pencils. The calculators students use in this unit should have the constant feature and should all be the same type. (While it is important that calculators be available at all times, they are listed on the first page of the lessons for which they are particularly important.) If possible, each group should have a container with all of these supplies available to use at their discretion.

Teacher Materials

- Sentence strips for "Number of the Week" bulletin board activity

- Materials for forming groups (Lesson 1)

- Sample "Group It!" booklet (Lesson 2)

- 3 baggies, each containing objects and a "Group It!" booklet, for each pair (use these baggies throughout the unit beginning with Lesson 2)

- "How Many Buttons in a Handful?" graph (Lesson 4)

- 2 half-sheets of 9″ × 12″ colored construction paper for you and each student (Lesson 5)

- "How Many Hands in Your Family?" graph (Lesson 6)

- *Free to Be a Family* by Marlo Thomas (New York and Toronto: Bantam, 1990) (Lesson 6)

- 9″ × 12″ colored construction paper for each student (Lesson 6)

- Overhead calculator or transparency of a calculator (Lessons 7, 8, and 9)

- Transparency of a Hundred Chart (Lessons 8 and 9)

- Transparency of "More Calculator Patterns" direction sheet (Lesson 9)

- *Ed Emberley's Great Thumbprint Drawing Book* by Ed Emberley (Boston and Toronto: Little, Brown and Company, 1977) (Lesson 10)

- Stamp pads (Lesson 10)

- Paper strips (Lesson 10)

- Thin-tip markers (Lesson 10)

- Access to soap, water, and paper towels (Lesson 10)

- Access to a copy machine (Lesson 10)

Student Materials

Each pair needs

- Counters (Lessons 1, 2, 5, and 6)

- Calculator with constant feature (Lessons 1, 2, 5, 6, 7, 8, 9, and 10)

- Baggie of 60–70 buttons (Lesson 3)

- Hundred Chart (Lesson 8)

Extension Materials

Each pair needs

- Calculator with constant feature (Lessons 5, 7, 8, and 9)

- Counters (Lessons 5 and 8)

- Hundred Chart (Lesson 9)

- Access to a stapler (Lesson 10)

- Drawing paper (Lesson 10)

Teaching Hints

- Prior to each lesson, think about open-ended questions you might ask to extend and probe the thinking of your students. Decide which Extensions to have ready for pairs or groups that finish early.

- Provide time for students to freely explore unfamiliar or infrequently used materials before each lesson.

- Have calculators available at all times during this unit for students to use when they choose. Throughout the unit, ask if any students have used calculators for their work and lead an informal discussion about their use.

- Some questions are suggested at the end of Lessons 2, 3, 5, 6, and 7 that may take students a considerable amount of time to explore. For example, in Lesson 3, students are asked to determine the total number of buttons taken in four handfuls. Extend the length of these lessons or have students investigate these questions during other class periods.

- In this unit, students are frequently asked to explain their thinking to their partners and to the class. Many lessons suggest that you ask follow-up questions to help students more fully explain or demonstrate their understanding. Recognize, however, that many students will have difficulty doing so, particularly at the beginning of the year. Provide many opportunities for students to talk about their thinking, to hear the thinking of others, and to use a variety of strategies to demonstrate their thinking, such as: drawing pictures, acting out, or verbalizing their solutions to a problem.

- Encourage students to organize their counting so that they can look at the objects and count them easily. For example, students might group objects on a sheet of paper and circle each group, or they might group objects into paper cups and count them.

- In Lessons 4 and 6, students are asked to respond to a graph as a way to collect data. These graphing experiences are intended to be informal and, therefore, include graphs with only one labeled axis. If appropriate, you may want to ask students to decide how the other axis could be labeled.

- After each lesson, review any Extensions students have not explored and decide whether to have students investigate these Extensions before going on to the next lesson.

Assessment Techniques

The informal assessment techniques suggested here will help you assess students' understanding of grouping and their ability to recognize and extend number patterns. Their purpose is not to determine mastery. Students' understanding will vary from experience to experience, particularly as they begin to construct their understanding.

Use the following assessment techniques throughout this unit and when indicated in a particular lesson. Before the lesson, prepare questions to ask yourself and your students that will help you assess students' understanding (many are suggested in the lessons). When you ask these questions, provide time for students to think, and resist the urge to teach. Probe students' thinking by asking open-ended questions that require them to explain further. Whenever possible, record students' responses. Compare students' responses over time to assess growth in their conceptual understanding.

Observe Individual Students Grouping and Counting

As students work, observe individuals and ask yourself the questions below.

> **Q. How does the student choose to group and count objects? Is the student able to count by 2s, 5s, and other groupings?**

Some students may not use the groupings to help them count. For example, students may group all of their objects by 2s, but when asked to count them will ignore the groupings and count by 1s. Some students may start counting by 2s, but lose the pattern. These students will need more experiences grouping, counting, extending, writing, and reading number patterns. Students construct an understanding of grouping and counting over time.

> **Q. Does the student understand that grouping and counting the same set by 1s, 2s, 3s, 10s, or any other grouping will produce the same total?**

Some students may believe that counting by 5s will give a different result than counting by 2s. These students will need more experiences counting the same objects by different groupings and comparing the results.

> **Q. Does the student continue the counting sequence far enough to be able to count all the objects that are chosen?**

Some students may choose to group large quantities by 2s, but are unable to extend the counting sequence. These students will need experiences grouping and counting large numbers of objects and should be encouraged to discuss ways to group the objects so that counting them is easier.

> **Q. Is the student able to recognize and extend a number pattern?**

Some students may not recognize a pattern in a counting sequence and may have trouble extending the pattern. For example, students may not recognize the number patterns they generate on their calculator, especially when they start the sequence at a number other than zero; for example, 1, 3, 5, 7, 9, and so on.

Student Writing

The focus of this unit is on having students demonstrate their ideas and explain their thinking verbally (see Teaching Hints, p. 4). In Lesson 4, students write statements about data on a graph.

How Many Groups?

Students explore the number of groups the class will have when divided into groups of two, three, four, and five students.

Class Builder Emphasis

In this lesson, students

- Develop a sense of unity as a class.
- Meet and work with their partner.
- Group and count.

Students add to their understanding that

- Quantities of objects and sets of data can be grouped and counted in various ways.
- Numbers can be composed and decomposed.

Social Emphasis

In this lesson, students

- Share the work.
- Explain their thinking.

Students continue to

- Develop appropriate group skills.
- Analyze the effect of behavior on others and on the group work.

Group Size: 2

Teacher Materials

- Materials for forming groups (see Before the Lesson)

Student Materials

Each pair needs

- Access to counters and calculators

■ Decide how you will form pairs to work together during the unit. (See Forming Groups, page xiii, for random-grouping suggestions.) Prepare any materials needed.

Notes

Write the total number of students in the class and make a table, such as the one below. As the lesson progresses, add the information students generate.

We have 31 students in our class.

Number of students in a group	Number of groups
2	14 groups of 2 and 1 group of 3
3	9 groups of 3 and 1 group of 4
4	7 groups of 4 and 1 group of 3

Teacher

Form pairs using the activity you have chosen. Be sure partners know each other's names.

Introduce the unit, explaining that students will work together to explore numbers and ways to group and count.

State that during the year students will work in many different groups and with many different classmates. Explain that you would like the class to help you find out how many groups there will be if the class is divided into groups of three, four, and five.

As a class, discuss the following questions:

Q. How many students are in our class?

Q. We divided our class into groups of two. How many pairs do we have? Do we have any groups with more than two students?

Q. If we had one more [one fewer] student in our class, how many pairs would we have? Two more [two fewer] students?

Ask students to help you find out how many groups you would have if you divided the class into groups of three. As a class, brainstorm some ways pairs might solve this problem, and list them where all can see. (Students might suggest strategies such as using counters, drawing pictures, or using a calculator.) Ask pairs to choose a strategy and decide how many groups of three the class would have.

Students

•• ••

•• ••

Notes	Teacher	Students

Notes

If pairs are having difficulty working together, help them analyze the situation by posing open-ended questions, such as:

Q. What seems to be causing problems?

Q. What have you tried?

Q. What else could you try? How might that help?

Teacher

Observe pairs and ask questions, such as:

Q. How are you sharing the work? Do you both think that it is a fair way? Why?

Q. How many groups of three do you think we will have? Why?

Students

●●

In pairs, students find the number of groups there would be if the class was divided into groups of three.

Notes

Encourage students to explain or demonstrate their strategies, and ask follow-up questions to probe their thinking.

Teacher

Have several pairs report their strategies for finding the number of groups there would be if the class was divided into groups of three. Ask questions, such as:

Q. How many groups of three would we have in our class? Would all groups have three students?

Q. How did you find the number of groups of three? Did any pair use a different strategy?

Q. Why can our class be divided into more pairs than groups of three?

Ask pairs to explore how many groups of four or of five the class would have. (Have pairs choose one of these group sizes to explore.)

Students

●● ●●
●● ●●

Notes

Observe how partners interact. Note positive interaction and any problems you might discuss as the class reflects on the lesson.

Teacher

Observe pairs and ask questions, such as:

Q. How did you find the number of groups of four [five] our class would have? Would all groups have four students?

Q. Why do you think there could be more groups of three than groups of four?

Students

●●

In pairs, students find the number of groups the class would have if divided into groups of four (or of five).

Mathematical Emphasis

Quantities of objects and sets of data can be grouped and counted in various ways.

Have pairs report their strategies and results for groups of four and groups of five. Ask questions to help students compare the results, such as:

Q. What group size gives us the greatest number of groups? Why? The fewest number of groups? Why?

Q. Why do you think there are more groups of three than groups of four?

Q. If we had two fewer students in our class, how many groups of two would we have? How many groups of three? How many groups of four? How many groups of five?

Help partners reflect on their interaction. Discuss questions, such as:

Social Emphasis

Analyze the effect of behavior on others and on the group work.

Q. How did you feel when you first heard you would be working with a partner? Were any of you worried? What worried you?

Q. What was something you liked about how you and your partner worked together? Why?

Provide more opportunities for pairs to get to know each other, such as those described in the Extension For Pairs That Finish Early.

Q. What were some problems you had? How did you feel? How did you solve them?

If appropriate, share some of your observations of the positive interaction and the problems you noted as pairs worked.

Extensions

For Pairs That Finish Early

■ Encourage pairs to take the time to get to know each other better. Have pairs share things about themselves, such as their favorite color, food, book, record, or TV program and why they like these things.

For the Next Day

■ Continue with the next lesson, "Group It!"

Group It!

Students explore different ways to group and count to determine the number of objects in a collection.

DAYS AHEAD
2

Mathematical Emphasis

In this lesson, students

- Group and count objects.

Students add to their understanding that

- Quantities of objects and sets of data can be grouped and counted in various ways.
- Numbers can be composed and decomposed.

Social Emphasis

In this lesson, students

- Use materials responsibly.
- Help each other.
- Share the work.

Students continue to

- Develop appropriate group skills.

Group Size: 2

Teacher Materials

- Sample "Group It!" booklet (see Before the Lesson)
- 3 baggies, each containing objects and a "Group It!" booklet, for each pair (see Before the Lesson)

Student Materials

Each pair needs

- Access to counters and calculators

Before the Lesson

- Make 3 "Group It!" booklets for each pair's baggies and a sample booklet to use for demonstration purposes. (See blackline master for directions.)

- For each pair, prepare 3 baggies, each with a different type of object (for example, buttons, ice cream sticks, or beans). Put one handful of objects in the first baggie, two in the second baggie, and three in the third baggie. Include a "Group It!" booklet in each baggie. Designate a place in the room for the baggies that is accessible to students. During the unit, the Extensions provide opportunities for pairs to continue to group and count these objects in different ways and to agree or disagree with the totals found by the original pair.

Notes	Teacher	Students
		●● ●●
You may wish to begin this lesson with a short activity that helps pairs become better acquainted.	Review that the focus of the unit is to group and count, to explore numbers, and to work together. Introduce this lesson by showing several baggies and wondering aloud about how many objects might be in each baggie and whether all the baggies have the same number of objects. Have students speculate with their partners, then discuss their thinking with the class.	●● ●●

Explain that each pair will get 3 baggies and that their job will be to group and count the number of objects in each baggie in a way other than counting by ones, then record the information on the "Group It!" booklet cover. Explain that during the next few weeks, other pairs will have an opportunity to group and count these objects using a different grouping, record their results inside the booklet, and record whether they agree or disagree with the first pair.

Stress the need to return each booklet to the appropriate baggie and to seal each baggie.

Show your sample "Group It!" booklet. Discuss the directions and model the activity with a partner and a baggie of objects.

Have pairs discuss what they learned about working with each other in the previous lesson that might help them work well today. If students do not bring up the subject, ask questions that help them discuss responsible ways to use the materials.

Distribute 3 baggies to each pair.

| **Notes** | **Teacher** | **Students** |

Observe students and note how they group and count the objects. Some students might group objects, but might not successfully count the groups because they do not know the number sequence. Others might ignore the groupings and count each item individually. These students will need many experiences counting objects by various groupings.

Mathematical Emphasis

Numbers can be composed and decomposed.

Pairs may need to use counters or calculators to help them solve these problems.

Provide sufficient time for students to explore these questions.

Observe pairs and, when appropriate, ask questions, such as:

Q. **How are you counting the objects? Show me.**

Q. **How many objects are in your baggie? Is that number closer to 50 or closer to 100? How do you know?**

Q. **How many groups or sets do you have? How many objects are left over?**

Q. **How are you sharing the work? Are you both happy with this? If not, how else could you share the work?**

Have pairs report the number of objects in their baggies. List the numbers where all can see. Point to different numbers and ask:

Q. **Is this number closer to 25, 50, or 100? How do you know?**

Help pairs reflect on the lesson by asking questions, such as:

Q. **How did you group your objects? Did anyone group their objects in a different way?**

Q. [Fiona and Byron] **counted** [52] **ice cream sticks. They counted by** [5s]. **How many groups of five did they have? How do you know?**

Q. [Willie and Shohei] **counted** [six] **groups of** [10] **beans, with** [two] **left over. How many beans are in their baggie?**

Q. [Chiyo and Natasha] **said they counted** [23] **plastic links.** [June and Bryant] **said they counted twice as many plastic links. What did** [June and Bryant] **mean? How many plastic links did** [June and Bryant] **count? How do you know?**

•• In pairs, students

1. Group and count the objects in the three baggies.

2. Record on the cover of the "Group It!" booklet.

3. Put the objects and the booklets back in each baggie and seal the baggie.

•• ••
•• ••

Notes	Teacher	Students

Social Emphasis
Develop appropriate group skills.

Q. How did you work together? What did you like about the way you worked together?

Q. How did your partner help you? How did you help your partner?

Q. How did you share the work? Was that fair? Why?

Q. Do you feel that you and your partner used the materials in a responsible way? Why?

Collect the baggies and put them in the designated place in the classroom. In order to model how to use the "Group It!" booklet and to continue to develop students' understanding of grouping and counting, have pairs investigate the activities in Extensions before going on to the next lesson.

Extensions

For Pairs That Finish Early

- Have pairs explore other ways to group and count the objects in one of their baggies. Students do not record in the "Group It!" booklet.

For the Next Day

- Select a baggie and read aloud how the first pair grouped and counted the objects and the total number found. Have students suggest another way to group the objects. Choose one of the suggestions, group and count the objects, and discuss how to record this grouping inside the "Group It!" booklet. Discuss what it means to agree or disagree. Hand out a baggie to each pair to group and count the objects using a different grouping. Have pairs record inside the booklet.

- Begin the "Number of the Week" bulletin board activity described in the Overview, p. 2.

Directions

Include a "Group It!" booklet in each baggie.

1. Copy and cut apart on the dotted lines.

2. Staple the "Group It!" cover on top of the four mini-pages of the booklet.

Group It!

Our names _____

_____

This baggie has _____
in it.

We grouped
by _____ .

Our total was _____ .

1

_____ _____
Our names

We grouped by _____ .

Our total was _____ .

We ☐ agree
☐ don't agree   with the first pair.

2

_____ _____
Our names

We grouped by _____ .

Our total was _____ .

We ☐ agree
☐ don't agree   with the first pair.

3

_____ _____
Our names

We grouped by _____ .

Our total was _____ .

We ☐ agree
☐ don't agree   with the first pair.

4

_____ _____
Our names

We grouped by _____ .

Our total was _____ .

We ☐ agree
☐ don't agree   with the first pair.

How Many Buttons?

Students group, count, and record the number of buttons that can be taken in a handful. Students will graph this data in the next lesson, "More Buttons."

DAYS AHEAD
1

Mathematical Emphasis

In this lesson, students

- Group and count objects.
- Record data.

Students add to their understanding that

- Quantities of objects and sets of data can be grouped and counted in various ways.
- Questions about our world can be asked, and data about those questions can be collected, organized, and analyzed.
- Numbers can be composed and decomposed.

Social Emphasis

In this lesson, students

- Agree on ways to group and count objects.
- Use materials responsibly.

Students continue to

- Develop appropriate group skills.
- Relate the values of fairness, caring, and responsibility to behavior.

Group Size: 2

Student Materials

Each pair needs

- Baggie of 60–70 buttons (see Before the Lesson)

Extension Materials

Each pair needs

- Access to baggies of objects (from Lesson 2)

■ Each pair will need a baggie containing 60 to 70 buttons. (Other manipulatives can be substituted for buttons, but all pairs need the same type of manipulative for this activity.)

Notes	Teacher	Students

Teacher

Introduce the lesson by telling a story, such as:

The other day I was putting my buttons away and decided to see how many buttons I could pick up in one handful. I took several handfuls and found that I could pick up between 40 and 57 buttons. Then I wondered why I didn't always pick up the same number of buttons in each handful.

Ask:

Q. Why do you think I didn't pick up the same number of buttons in each handful?

Q. If each student picks up a handful of buttons, do you think all of us will pick up the same number of buttons? Why?

Explain that pairs will gather data for four handfuls. State that in the next lesson students will graph the data they collect, so they will need to keep a record of the number of buttons in each handful. Suggest that one partner take a handful, then the pair group, count, and record the number of buttons in the handful. Have pairs continue this procedure, alternating which partner takes the handful. Ask pairs to use a different grouping to count each handful.

With a student as your partner, demonstrate the activity, and discuss ways partners might work cooperatively.

Notes

Consider having students fold a piece of paper into fourths and then number each section to represent each handful. Students can then record their data.

Model ways to work cooperatively with your partner, such as discussing with your partner how you might group the buttons and agreeing on a way to group and count the buttons. Ask the class what you and your partner did that helped you work well together.

Notes	**Teacher**	**Students**

Observe groups and ask yourself the following questions:

Q. How are pairs choosing to group and count the buttons? Are they able to count by 2s, 3s, 5s, and so on? How far can they count accurately by these groupings?

Q. Do pairs understand that counting the same set by different groupings will yield the same total?

Observe pairs working and, when appropriate, ask questions, such as:

Q. By what grouping are you counting your handful of buttons? How many groups do you have? How many buttons are left over? How many are there all together?

Q. How many buttons would you have if you added [1] more group? How many would you have if you took away [1] group? How do you know?

Q. Look at your record of the number of buttons taken in each handful. Which handful is closer to 50 buttons? How do you know?

●● In pairs, students

1. Take turns taking a handful of buttons and then agree on how to group and count them, using a different grouping for each handful.

2. Record the number of buttons in each handful.

3. Repeat, using a different grouping, for a total of four handfuls.

Mathematical Emphasis

Numbers can be composed and decomposed.

A cooperative structure such as "Turn to Your Partner" (see p. xii) provides opportunities for all students to be involved in the discussion.

Provide sufficient time for students to explore these questions.

Students may need to use the buttons to help them solve these problems.

Ask several pairs to share how they grouped and counted their handfuls. First in pairs, then as a class, discuss questions, such as:

Q. If you had a handful of 36 buttons, how many sets of 10 could you make? Would you have any left over?

Q. If you took that same set of 36 buttons and grouped it into sets of 5, how many sets would you have? How do you know? Would you have any left over? How do you know? What if you grouped them into sets of 2?

Q. If you had 4 sets of 5 buttons and 3 buttons left over, how many buttons would you have? How many would you have if you added 3 more sets of 5?

Q. Look at the number of buttons in one handful. If you had picked up half as many buttons, about how many would you have in that handful? How do you know?

Q. Look at your data. Did you pick up more or less than 100 buttons in all four handfuls? How do you know?

Q. How is this lesson similar to previous lessons?

●● ●●

●● ●●

Notes	Teacher	Students

Social Emphasis
Relate the values of fairness, caring, and responsibility to behavior.

Help students reflect on their work together by asking questions, such as:

•• ••

•• ••

Q. What went well as you worked together? What problems did you have?

Q. What would you do differently the next time?

Q. How did you make decisions?

Q. What do you notice about how our class handled the materials today? What would you suggest as responsible ways to handle the materials?

Collect students' record sheets or have pairs save them for the next lesson.

Extensions

For Pairs That Finish Early

■ Have pairs choose a "Group It!" baggie (from Lesson 2). Have pairs group and count the objects in the baggie using a grouping that previous pairs haven't tried for that baggie, and record the results inside the booklet in the baggie.

For the Next Day

■ Continue with the "Number of the Week" bulletin board activity described in the Overview, p. 2.

■ Continue with the next lesson, "More Buttons."

More Buttons

Students graph and analyze data collected during "How Many Buttons?" and write several statements about the data.

DAYS AHEAD
1

Mathematical Emphasis

In this lesson, students

- Graph and interpret data.
- Write statements about data.

Students add to their understanding that

- Questions about our world can be asked, and data about those questions can be collected, organized, and analyzed.
- Numbers can be used to describe quantities.

Social Emphasis

In this lesson, students

- Explain their thinking.
- Listen to others.

Students continue to

- Develop appropriate group skills.
- Relate the values of fairness, caring, and responsibility to behavior.

Group Size: 2

Teacher Materials

- "How Many Buttons in a Handful?" graph (see Before the Lesson)
- Markers

Student Materials

Each pair needs

- Record sheet with their data (from Lesson 3)

Extension Materials

Each pair needs

- Access to baggies of objects (from Lesson 2)

How many buttons in a handful?

15-19 | 20-24 | 25-29 | 30-34 | 35-39 | 40-44 | 45-49 | 50-54 | 55-59 | 60-64

Stephanie A.J.
9 students picked up from 35 to 39 buttons.

■ Make the following graph on a large sheet of paper and post.

◎◎ How Many Buttons in a Handful? ◎⑪									
15-19	20-24	25-29	30-34	35-39	40-44	45-49	50-54	55-59	60-64

Number of Buttons

Notes

Pause at various times as students are recording, and discuss the data collected to that point.

Teacher

Introduce the lesson by asking students what they discovered in the previous lesson. Ask questions, such as:

Q. What did you discover about the number of buttons you could pick up in one handful?

Q. How did you group and count the buttons?

Direct students' attention to the graph and discuss. Ask questions, such as:

Q. If I want to show a handful that had 42 buttons, which box would I color in? Why?

Q. If this box (point to a box) **were colored in, what would we know?**

Ask pairs to look at the data they collected in the previous lesson, "How Many Buttons?" Have them discuss where they would record the number of buttons in each handful and how to divide the work. Ask pairs to record their data on the "How Many Buttons in a Handful?" graph.

Students

●● ●●

●● ●●

•• ••

•• ••

Notes

Mathematical Emphasis

Questions about our world can be asked, and data about those questions can be collected, organized, and analyzed.

A cooperative structure such as "Turn to Your Partner" (see p. xii) can provide opportunities for all students to be involved in the discussion.

Teacher

After all pairs have graphed their data, discuss the data on the graph. Ask questions, such as:

Q. **What do you notice about the data?**

Q. **In which columns are the data clumped?**

Q. **Are there any columns that contain no data? Why do you think that has happened? Are the data spread out? Why do you think that has happened?**

Q. **If a student from another second grade classroom were to pick up a handful of buttons, about how many buttons do you think would be in the handful? Why?**

Explain that pairs are to write statements about the data. Model this by writing the following statement, using data from the completed graph, where all can see:

> [15] **of the handfuls had from** [35] **to** [39] **buttons.**

Read the statement aloud. Ask whether students agree or disagree and encourage students to explain their thinking.

Model writing another statement about the data, such as:

> **There are more handfuls in the [40–44] column than in any other column.**

Again, ask students whether they agree or disagree and why.

Ask pairs to think of a statement they could make about the data. Have two pairs share their statements with the class, and write these statements where all can see. Encourage students to explain why they agree or disagree with the statements.

Ask pairs to write one or two statements about the data.

Notes	**Teacher**	**Students**

Observe how partners interact. Note positive interaction and any problems you might discuss as the class reflects on the lesson.

Observe pairs and, when appropriate, ask questions, such as:

Q. **How are you showing your partner that you are listening to his or her ideas?**

Q. **How are you making sure your partner understands your ideas?**

Q. **How are you and your partner making sure the statements you are writing are true?**

●●

In pairs, students write one or two statements about the data.

Have several pairs share their statements about the data. Encourage students to explain why they agree or disagree with the statements.

●● ●●

●● ●●

Help students reflect on the lesson by asking questions, such as:

Social Emphasis
Relate the values of fairness, caring, and responsibility to behavior.

Q. **What compliments would you give yourselves about how you worked today?**

Q. **In what ways did you help your partner? How did you feel? In what ways did your partner help you? How did you feel?**

Q. **How did your record sheet help you remember your data from the previous lesson?**

If appropriate, share some of your observations of the positive interaction and the problems you noted as pairs worked.

Extensions

For Pairs That Finish Early

■ Have pairs choose a "Group It!" baggie (from Lesson 2) that they have not yet explored.

For the Next Day

■ Continue with the "Number of the Week" bulletin board activity described in the Overview, p. 2.

Friendship Chain

Students use their own strategy to determine the number of sheets of paper needed to make a Friendship Chain. They then help each other trace their hands, cut out the traced hands, and glue the hands together to make a chain. This lesson may take more than one class period.

Mathematical Emphasis

In this lesson, students

- Compute informally.
- Group and count by twos.

Students add to their understanding that

- Quantities of objects and sets of data can be grouped and counted in various ways.
- Operations can be carried out in a variety of ways.
- Numbers can be used to describe quantities.

Social Emphasis

In this lesson, students

- Help each other.
- Include everyone.

Students continue to

- Develop appropriate group skills.
- Analyze the effect of behavior on others and on the group work.

Group Size: 4

Teacher Materials

- 2 half-sheets of 9″ × 12″ colored construction paper for you and each student

Student Materials

Each group of four needs

- Scissors
- Glue stick
- Access to counters and calculators

Extension Materials

Each group of four needs

- Access to counters and calculators

Combine pairs to form groups of four. Discuss the number of groups of four in the class.

Introduce the lesson by asking students to examine their hands. Facilitate a discussion about the features of their hands and how we use our hands to communicate. (For example, we shake hands as a sign of greeting and friendship.) Ask students to greet the others in their group by shaking hands.

Explain that the class will create a symbol of their friendship by making a paper chain of their hands joined together. Explain that students will trace around both their hands on paper, cut out the hand shapes, and glue them to form a chain.

Show a half-sheet of construction paper to the students. First in groups, then as a class, discuss:

Q. How many sheets of paper this size will you need to trace all the hands in your group if each hand is traced on a separate sheet? How do you know?

Wonder aloud about the number of sheets of paper that the class will need if you and all students in the class trace their hands on separate sheets of paper. Explain that groups will solve this problem.

Social Emphasis
Develop appropriate group skills.

Facilitate a discussion about what might help group members work well together, and discuss why it is important to include everyone. Ask questions, such as:

Q. How might working in a group of four be different from working as a pair?

Q. What have you learned about working together in pairs that might help you in your group of four?

Q. How can you make sure everyone in your group is included? Why is that important?

Encourage groups to choose their own strategy to determine the number of sheets of paper needed. For example, groups may count by 2s, use mental computation, use a calculator, use counters, or choose another strategy or combination of strategies.

If students have trouble working together, open-ended questions may help them analyze the problem. Ask questions, such as:

Q. What seems to be causing problems?
Q. What might you do about that?
Q. How might that help? How is that a fair way to work?

As you observe students, ask yourself questions, such as:

Q. What strategies do students use to solve the problem? Can they describe those strategies?

Observe groups working and, when appropriate, ask questions, such as:

Q. Why do you think your solution is reasonable?

Q. How are you making sure everyone is getting a chance to share his or her ideas?

Q. How are you making sure everyone is included?

In groups, students determine the number of sheets of paper needed for all students and the teacher to trace their hands, if each hand is traced on a separate sheet of paper.

Notes	Teacher	Students

Mathematical Emphasis

Operations can be carried out in a variety of ways.

A cooperative structure such as "Think, Pair, Share" (see p. xii) can provide opportunities for all students to reflect on a problem and discuss their thinking.

Provide sufficient time for students to explain their strategies, for the class to discuss the strategies, and for the class to try each other's strategies.

Ask several groups to share the strategies they used to determine the number of sheets of paper needed. Ask questions, such as:

Q. **What strategy did your group use to find the number of sheets of paper needed to trace each hand in the class?**

Q. **Did any group use a different strategy?**

Q. **When [Juanita] reported, she said that her group solved the problem by using one cube for each of the [32] students and one cube for me** (the teacher). **Each cube represented two hands, so her group counted two for each cube. They think we will need [66] sheets of paper. Do you agree or disagree with this strategy? Let's try this strategy.**

Q. **[John] said that his group solved the problem by counting [8] groups in the class and adding [8] hands for each group [8] times. They knew that 8 + 8 = 16. Then they used their calculator to add 16 + 16 + 16 + 16, and they got 64. They added 2 sheets for me** (the teacher) **and 4 extra sheets in case students made mistakes, for a total of 70 sheets. Do you agree or disagree with their solution? Let's try this strategy. Why did they add 16 four times and not eight times?**

Q. **If we had five fewer students in our class, how many sheets of paper would we need? How do you know?**

Q. **Suppose we had twice as many students in our class. How many sheets of paper would we need? How do you know?**

Distribute the construction paper.

Notes	**Teacher**	**Students**

Notes

See the illustration on the front page of this lesson for an example of how the chain might look.

Teacher

Have students help each other trace their hands (one hand per half-sheet of paper), cut them out, and glue them together with other hands in their group.

Students

●● In groups, students

1. Help each other trace their hands.

2. Cut out their hand shapes and make a group chain.

Have the groups glue their chains together to make a class Friendship Chain and display.

●● ●●
●● ●●
●● ●●

Social Emphasis
Analyze the effect of behavior on others and on the group work.

As a class, reflect on the lesson and discuss the group work. Ask questions, such as:

Q. What did you do to help your group?

Q. Did anyone feel that he or she was left out of the work? What did you do? Did it work? What did your group do?

Q. How was this lesson similar to or different from other lessons in this unit?

Extensions

For Groups That Finish Early

■ Ask groups to estimate whether they would need more or less than 500 sheets of paper to make a Friendship Chain that included all the second grade students in the school. Have groups discuss their reasons for their estimates.

■ Ask groups to determine the number of fingers in the class.

For the Next Day

■ Continue with the "Number of the Week" bulletin board activity described in the Overview, p. 2.

■ Continue with the next lesson, "Family Friendship Chain."

Family Friendship Chain

Students determine the number of hands in their families, plot this information on a class graph, and discuss the data on the graph. This lesson will take more than one class period.

DAYS AHEAD
1

Mathematical Emphasis

In this lesson, students

- Collect, organize, and analyze data.
- Compute informally.

Students add to their understanding that

- Questions about our world can be asked, and data about those questions can be collected, organized, and analyzed.
- Operations can be carried out in a variety of ways.

Social Emphasis

In this lesson, students

- Help each other.
- Explain their thinking.
- Listen to each other.

Students continue to

- Develop appropriate group skills.
- Analyze the effect of behavior on others and on the group work.

Group Size: 2

Teacher Materials

- "How Many Hands in Your Family?" graph (see Before the Lesson)
- Markers
- *Free to Be a Family* (see Before the Lesson)
- 9" × 12" colored construction paper (see Before the Lesson)

Student Materials

Each pair needs

- Access to counters and calculators

Extension Materials

Each pair needs

- Scissors
- Glue stick

■ Make the following graph on a large piece of paper and post.

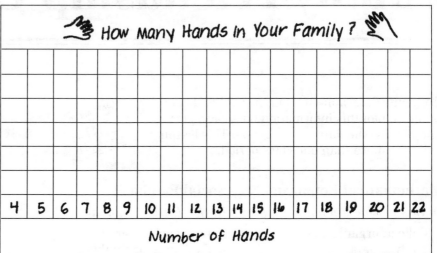

■ If possible, locate a copy of *Free to Be a Family* by Marlo Thomas (New York and Toronto: Bantam, 1990). Consider reading this aloud to foster a discussion about the diversity of families.

■ Determine the quantity of 9″ × 12″ colored construction paper to provide students to take home at the end of the lesson in order to trace the hands of each member of their families.

Notes	Teacher	Students

Discuss the previous lesson and ask students how many hands are in the class Friendship Chain.

Wonder aloud about how many hands would be in a Friendship Chain that included all the students and their families and you and your family. Discuss the term *immediate family* and the diversity of families. Ask questions, such as:

This might be a good time to read and discuss *Free to Be a Family*, if available.

Q. There are many types of families. Some have one child, some have many children. Some have one adult, some have many adults. What are some types of families that you know?

Explain that partners will discuss the number of people in their immediate families and help each other find how many hands are in each of their families, including themselves. Direct students' attention to the graph and discuss questions, such as:

Notes	Teacher	Students
	Q. If there are five people in your family, including you, how many hands would there probably be? How do you know? Where would you mark the graph?	•• •• •• ••
	Q. If this box (point to a box) were filled in, what would it mean?	
	Q. If two boxes were filled in the same column (point to two boxes in the same column), what would it mean?	
	Q. If three boxes were filled in this column (point to a column), what would it mean?	
	To model, discuss the number of people and the number of hands in your own family and mark the graph. Explain that each student will record the number of hands in his or her immediate family.	

| ASSESSMENT
 Observe how partners interact. Note positive interaction and any problems you might discuss as the class reflects on the lesson.

 If students are waiting to plot their data or are waiting for others to finish, have them tell each other more about themselves. | **O**bserve pairs working and ask questions, such as:

 Q. How are you helping each other?

 Q. How are you figuring out the number of hands in your family?

 Q. What will you record on the graph? Why? | ••   In pairs, students

 1. Help each other determine the number of hands in their immediate families.

 2. Individually mark the class graph. |

| **Mathematical Emphasis**
 Questions about our world can be asked, and data about those questions can be collected, organized, and analyzed. | First in pairs, and then as a class, discuss questions such as:

 Q. How did you determine the number of hands in your family?

 Q. When you look at the graph, what do you notice about the data?

 Q. In which columns are the data clumped? | •• ••
 •• •• |

Q. Are there any columns that contain no data? Why do you think that has happened? Are the data spread out? Why do you think that happened?

•• ••

•• ••

Q. What does this column of data tell us? (Point to one of the columns. It could mean that [5] students have [8] hands in their families.)

Students may need to use calculators to help them solve this problem.

Provide sufficient time for students to explore these questions.

Q. Will we need more or less than 200 sheets of paper if each student in the class traced their family hands? How do you know?

Help students reflect on the lesson. Ask questions, such as:

Social Emphasis

Analyze the effect of behavior on others and on the group work.

Q. How did having a partner help you today?

Q. What did you do to help your partner?

If appropriate, discuss some of your observations of the group work.

Make hands for the members of your family to include in the Family Friendship Chain that will be made during the Extension For the Next Day.

Distribute colored construction paper and ask students to trace the hands of each family member at home.

Extensions

For Pairs That Finish Early

■ Ask pairs to write statements about the data on the graph.

For the Next Day

■ Have pairs help each other cut out the hand tracings of their family members. Put all the hand shapes together, including those for your own family, to make a Family Friendship Chain. Discuss the number of hands in the chain, and have students compare this number with the number of hands in the class Friendship Chain.

■ Ask pairs to create a different question about families. Have pairs share their questions and, as a class, decide on one of the questions that students would like to investigate. Have pairs collect data about the question. As a class, decide how to organize the data on a graph. Ask pairs to analyze the data and write statements about the data on the graph. This Extension will take more than one class period.

Count with Calculators

Students explore number patterns on their calculators. Pairs then find numbers that, when added repeatedly, will reach the target number 100. This lesson may take more than one class period.

DAYS AHEAD
4

Mathematical Emphasis

In this lesson, students

■ Explore calculators.
■ Look for patterns.

Students add to their understanding that

■ Once a rule to generate a pattern has been identified, the pattern can usually be extended.
■ Numbers can be composed and decomposed.

Social Emphasis

In this lesson, students

■ Share the work.
■ Share materials.
■ Explain their thinking.

Students continue to

■ Develop appropriate group skills.
■ Relate the values of fairness, caring, and responsibility to behavior.

Group Size: 2

Teacher Materials

■ Overhead calculator or a transparency of a calculator similar to students' calculators

Student Materials

Each pair needs

■ Calculator with constant feature (all calculators should be the same type)

Extension Materials

Each pair needs

■ Calculator

Leda Demetrius
3, 6, 9, 12,

- If students' previous experience with calculators has been limited, provide time for them to individually explore the calculator before this lesson. Have pairs discuss what they discovered about the calculator.

- You might wish to experiment beforehand using the calculator to count in the manner suggested in this lesson.

Notes	Teacher	Students

Teacher

Facilitate a discussion about the mathematics students have explored in the unit. Ask questions, such as:

Q. What have you explored about grouping and counting in previous lessons?

Q. By what numbers have you been grouping and counting?

As a class, count aloud by various groupings. (For example, by 2s, 5s, 10s, and so on. It is not necessary to count to 100.)

Explain that today students will continue to investigate grouping and counting by exploring how to use calculators to count by different numbers. Ask:

Q. How might we count using the calculator?

If students have already discovered how to count on the calculator, have a student use the overhead calculator or transparency to demonstrate. Ask the class to follow the student's directions. If students have not discovered how to count using the calculator, model by asking pairs to:

Notes

As you give directions, use an overhead calculator or a transparency of a calculator to show students which keys to press.

- clear the calculator
- press 2
- press +
- press =

Ask:

Q. What number is in the calculator window? [2]

Ask pairs to press = again. Ask:

●● ●●

●● ●●

Q. **What number is in the calculator window?** [4]

Q. **If we press = again, what number will we see in the calculator window?** [6] **Why?**

Q. **If we continue to press =, what numbers will we see in the window?** [8, 10, 12, and so on] **Why? By what number are we counting?** [2]

For example, if 5, +, = is entered, the calculator counts by 5s. In this case, the hidden counter is 5.

Explain that when you enter a number and press + and then press =, the number becomes a "hidden counter."

Ask pairs to try a hidden counter of their own on their calculator. After a few minutes, discuss questions, such as:

Mathematical Emphasis

Once a rule to generate a pattern has been identified, the pattern can usually be extended.

Q. **What number did you and your partner use as your hidden counter?**

Q. **What numbers did you see in your calculator window?**

Q. **What patterns do you notice?**

First in pairs, and then as a class, discuss questions, such as:

Q. **If you use 2 as your hidden counter, do you think you would be able to reach 100 on your calculator? Why?**

Ask pairs to choose two numbers from 1 through 9, predict whether they can reach the target number 100 using these numbers as hidden counters, and then try both hidden counters on their calculators, keeping track of the number of times they press = to reach 100. Ask students to read aloud each number as it appears in the calculator window.

Notes	Teacher	Students

Notes

Encourage students to pay close attention to the numbers as they appear in the calculator window and read the numbers to their partners.

Teacher

Observe pairs working and, when appropriate, ask questions, such as:

Q. **What are you discovering?**

Q. **How are you making sure you both understand what is happening? Why is that important?**

Q. **How are you sharing the work?**

Q. **How are you keeping a record of the number of times you press =?**

Students

••   In pairs, students

1. Choose two numbers from 1 through 9.

2. Predict whether those numbers, when used as hidden counters, will reach the target number 100.

3. Try both numbers as hidden counters on their calculator, keeping track of the number of times they press = to reach 100.

Notes

As students report their findings, list them on a chart, and then ask:

Q. What patterns and relationships do you notice?

Counter	Number of times
1	100
2	50
4	25
5	20
10	?

Provide time for pairs to explore larger numbers to use as counters and then to reflect on the patterns and relationships. A completed chart might look like this:

Counter	Number of times
1	100
2	50
4	25
5	20
10	10
20	5
25	4
50	2
100	1

Teacher

First in pairs, then as a class, discuss questions, such as:

Q. **Which numbers from 1 through 9, when added repeatedly, reached 100? When using 1 as your counter, how many times would you press = to reach 100? When using 2 as your counter, how many times would you press = to reach 100? How many times for 4? 5?**

Q. **Which numbers, when added repeatedly, did not reach 100? Why do you think they did not?**

Q. **If you use 10 as your counter, do you think you will reach 100 exactly? Why?**

Q. **What numbers larger than 10 might reach 100 exactly?**

Have pairs explore numbers 10 and larger to use as counters.

Students

••   ••

••   ••

Notes	Teacher	Students

Teacher

Help students reflect on their work together by asking questions, such as:

Q. **What went well for you and your partner? What did you do that helped you work well together?**

Q. **How did you keep track of the number of times you pressed =? How did that work?**

Q. **How did you share the calculator? Did you think that was fair? Why? Would you want to do it the same way again? If not, what would you do differently?**

To help students continue to develop their understanding of number patterns and computation, have pairs investigate the activities in Extensions before going on to the next lesson.

Notes

Social Emphasis

Relate the values of fairness, caring, and responsibility to behavior.

Extensions

For Pairs That Finish Early

- Have pairs explore whether the same numbers that reached 100, when added repeatedly, will reach 200 and whether there are any other numbers that, when added repeatedly, will reach 200.

For the Next Day

- Have pairs explore subtraction and number patterns on their calculator by repeatedly subtracting a number from 100. For example:

  - clear the calculator
  - enter 100
  - press –
  - press 5
  - press = = = and so on

  The calculator window will show 100, 95, 90, and so on.

- Continue with the "Number of the Week" bulletin board activity described in the Overview, p. 2.

Calculator Patterns

Students use calculators and Hundred Charts to explore number patterns.

Mathematical Emphasis

In this lesson, students

- Explore the calculator.
- Look for patterns.

Students add to their understanding that

- Numbers can be composed and decomposed.
- Once a rule to generate a pattern has been identified, the pattern can usually be extended.

Social Emphasis

In this lesson, students

- Share the work.
- Share materials.
- Explain their thinking.

Students continue to

- Develop appropriate group skills.
- Analyze the effect of behavior on others and on the group work.

Group Size: 2

Teacher Materials

- Overhead calculator or a transparency of a calculator
- Transparency of a Hundred Chart

Student Materials

Each pair needs

- Calculator
- Hundred Chart

Extension Materials

Each pair needs

- Access to baggies of objects (from Lesson 2)
- Access to counters and calculators

Notes	Teacher	Students

Teacher

As a class, discuss the previous lesson and what students learned about grouping, counting, and number patterns. Explain that pairs will use the calculator to continue exploring number patterns.

Show the Hundred Chart transparency. First in pairs, then as a class, discuss the chart and ask questions, such as:

Q. What patterns do you notice?

State that pairs will count on their calculator and circle the numbers on the Hundred Chart that appear in the calculator window. Write the following directions where all can see and discuss:

- clear the calculator $\boxed{C}$
- choose a number from 1 through 9
- press that number $\boxed{3}$
- press $\boxed{+}$
- press $\boxed{=}$
- continue to press $\boxed{=}$ and circle each number you see in the calculator window on the Hundred Chart

Use an overhead calculator or a transparency of a calculator to show students which keys to press as you give the class directions.

Demonstrate with the following example:

- clear the calculator
- press 2
- press +
- press = = = = and so on

As you press =, demonstrate circling the number you see in the calculator window on the Hundred Chart transparency (2, 4, 6, 8, and so on).

Ask pairs what they learned in the previous lessons that will help them work well together. Ask questions, such as:

Q. What did you like about the way you and your partner worked together in the previous lessons?

Social Emphasis
Develop appropriate group skills.

Notes	Teacher	Students
	Q. **What problems have you had? How might you avoid them today?**	•• ••
	Q. **How did you share the calculator in the previous lesson? Were you happy with this method? What else might you try?**	•• ••
	Observe pairs working and, when appropriate, ask questions, such as:	•• In pairs, students
		1. Clear the calculator
	Q. **What are you and your partner discovering?**	2. Enter a number from 1 through 9
	Q. **How are you sharing the work? How are you sharing the calculator? How is sharing helping you work together? If not, what else might you do?**	3. Press +
		4. Press =
		5. Circle the number displayed each time they press = on their Hundred Chart

Notes	Teacher	Students
Mathematical Emphasis Once a rule to generate a pattern has been identified, the pattern can usually be extended.	**D**isplay five or six of the pairs' Hundred Charts where all can see. Ask questions, such as: Q. **What patterns do you notice?** Q. **Are any of these charts the same? How?** Q. **Based on this pattern** (point to one of the Hundred Charts)**, what number would come next in the sequence?** (For example, 94, 98, ___, ___, and so on.)	•• •• •• ••

Social Emphasis

Analyze the effect of behavior on others and on the group work.

Help students reflect on their work with their partner by asking questions, such as:

•• ••

•• ••

Q. **What went well for you and your partner? What did you do that helped you work well together?**

Q. **Think to yourself what kind of a partner you were today. Did you help your pair? How? Did your behavior cause a problem for your pair? What kind of a partner do you want to be?**

To help students continue to develop their understanding of number patterns and grouping, have pairs investigate the activities in Extensions before going on to the next lesson.

Extensions

For Pairs That Finish Early

■ Have pairs choose a "Group It!" baggie (from Lesson 2), group the objects in the baggies by a different grouping, and use the calculator to count the groups. Have pairs record their results inside the booklet in the baggie.

For the Next Day

■ As a class, list things that come in pairs, things that come in 3s, things that come in 4s, things that come in 5s, and things that come in 10s; for example, shoes, sides of a triangle, leaves on a four-leaf clover, and so on. Pick one of the numbers and model making a chart that shows the number pattern that develops when counting multiples of these objects. For example, for 3s you might make a chart showing the number of sides on triangles, such as:

Number of triangles	Number of sides
1	3
2	6
3	9
.	.
.	.
.	.

Have pairs pick a number and make a chart showing the number pattern. Students may choose to draw pictures or use counters to help them determine the number pattern. For example, students might draw horses and count their legs to develop a chart for multiples of four.

Hundred Chart

1	2	3	4	5	6	7	8	9	10
11	12	13	14	15	16	17	18	19	20
21	22	23	24	25	26	27	28	29	30
31	32	33	34	35	36	37	38	39	40
41	42	43	44	45	46	47	48	49	50
51	52	53	54	55	56	57	58	59	60
61	62	63	64	65	66	67	68	69	70
71	72	73	74	75	76	77	78	79	80
81	82	83	84	85	86	87	88	89	90
91	92	93	94	95	96	97	98	99	100

More Calculator Patterns

Students continue to find and compare number patterns on a calculator.

Mathematical Emphasis

In this lesson, students

- Explore the calculator.
- Look for patterns.

Students add to their understanding that

- Numbers can be composed and decomposed.
- The same pattern can occur in a variety of settings.
- Once a rule to generate a pattern has been identified, the pattern can usually be extended.

Social Emphasis

In this lesson, students

- Share the work.
- Share materials.
- Explain their thinking.

Students continue to

- Develop appropriate group skills.
- Relate the values of fairness, caring, and responsibility to behavior.

Group Size: 2

Teacher Materials

- Overhead calculator or transparency of a calculator
- Transparency of "More Calculator Patterns" direction sheet
- Transparency of Hundred Chart (see Lesson 8)

Student Materials

Each pair needs

- Calculator

Extension Materials

Each pair needs

- Hundred Chart (see Lesson 8)
- Calculator

Notes	Teacher	Students

Throughout this unit students have been asked to count by various groupings. This repetition is important for students to help them internalize the various counting sequences.

Show the Hundred Chart transparency and introduce the lesson by asking students to discuss different ways they can count. As a class, count aloud by various groupings. (For example, the class might count by 2s, 5s, 10s, and so on. It is not necessary to count to 100.) As students say a number, point to it on the Hundred Chart transparency.

Explain that in the previous calculator lessons students started at 0 and counted by 2s, 5s, 10s, and so on. Say that today pairs will count on their calculators starting with a number other than 0.

Have pairs

- clear the calculator
- press 1
- press +
- press 4
- press =

As you give directions, use an overhead calculator or a transparency of a calculator to show students which keys to press.

Ask:

Q. What number do you see in the calculator window? [5]

Have pairs press =. Ask:

Q. What number do you see in the calculator window? [9] **If we press = again, what number will you see in the calculator window?** [13] **How do you know?**

Have pairs press = again. Ask:

Q. What number is in the window? [13] **If we press = again, what number will the calculator show? Why?**

Have pairs press = again. Ask:

Q. What number is in the calculator window? [17]

Q. If you press = = =, what number will be displayed in the calculator window? [29] **How do you know?**

Q. By what number are we counting? [4] **How do you know?**

Mathematical Emphasis

Once a rule to generate a pattern has been identified, the pattern can usually be extended.

Notes	Teacher	Students
For example, students might clear their calculators, start with 1, and record 1. If their counter is 2, they would press + and 2, but not record 2. (Emphasize that students should not record the counter.) They would then press = and record the number in the window (3). Each time they pressed =, they would record the number displayed in their calculator window (5, 7, 9, 11, …).	Show the "More Calculator Patterns" transparency and discuss the directions. Explain that pairs will find number patterns beginning at any number from 1 through 9 and using a counter from 1 through 9. Model several examples with the class. (Remember to record the first number in the sequence and each following number, but not the counter.)	•• •• •• ••

When you ask students what they think will happen, notice whether they can see the pattern and extend it.	Observe pairs and, when appropriate, ask questions, such as: Q. If you press = twice, what number do you think will be displayed in the calculator window? Why? Try it.	•• In pairs, students generate number patterns on their calculator and record and discuss the patterns.

Mathematical Emphasis The same pattern can occur in a variety of settings.	Ask two or three pairs to share one of their number patterns with the class. As pairs share their patterns, write them where all can see and ask questions, such as: Q. What pattern(s) do you notice? Q. By what number are we counting in each of the number patterns? Q. Based on the pattern in this sequence (point to a number pattern), what number would come next? (For example, 1, 3, 5, 7, 9, _?_) Q. What patterns did you find when you counted by [3s]? Did any other pair discover a different pattern when you counted by [3s]? Why?	•• •• •• ••

Notes	Teacher	Students

Social Emphasis
Relate the values of fairness, caring, and responsibility to behavior.

Help students reflect on how they worked together by asking questions, such as:

Q. How did you share the work? Was that fair? Why?

Q. How did you and your partner work responsibly?

Extensions

For Pairs That Finish Early

■ Have pairs choose one of the number patterns they explored on their calculator and circle the numbers on a Hundred Chart. Ask pairs to describe the resulting patterns.

For the Next Day

■ Explain how to play Find That Counter.

1. One partner clears the calculator and enters the following:
   ■ a secret number (any number from 1 through 9)
   ■ +
   ■ = =
   (For example, 5, +, =, =.)

2. The other partner takes the calculator and tries to guess the hidden counter by continuing to press = and looking at the numbers displayed in the calculator window.

More Calculator Patterns
Directions

1. Clear the calculator.

2. Enter a number from 1 through 9.

3. Record the number you entered.

4. Press $\boxed{+}$.

5. Enter a number from 1 through 9. (Do not record.)

6. Press $\boxed{=}$.

7. Record the number you see in your calculator window.

8. Press $\boxed{=}$.

9. Record the number you see in your calculator window.

10. Continue to press $\boxed{=}$ and record the numbers you see in your calculator window.

Autograph Books

Students reflect on their work together in this unit and create a page for an autograph book by making pictures with their fingerprints. This lesson will take more than one class period.

Transition Emphasis

In this lesson, students

- Reflect on how they worked together.
- Thank each other and say good-bye.
- Count by tens.
- Compute informally.

Students add to their understanding that

- Quantities of objects and sets of data can be grouped and counted in various ways.
- Operations can be carried out in a variety of ways.

Social Emphasis

In this lesson, students

- Help each other.
- Share materials.
- Use materials responsibly.

Students continue to

- Develop appropriate group skills.
- Analyze the effect of behavior on others and on the group work.

Group Size: 2

Teacher Materials

- *Ed Emberley's Great Thumbprint Drawing Book* (see Before the Lesson)
- Stamp pads (see Before the Lesson)
- Paper strips (see Before the Lesson)
- Thin-tip markers
- Access to soap, water, and paper towels
- Access to a copy machine (see Before the Lesson)

Student Materials

Each pair needs

- Thin-tip markers
- Access to a calculator

Extension Materials

Each pair needs

- Drawing paper
- Markers
- Access to a stapler

■ In this lesson, students print their fingerprints on strips of paper and then create pictures using the fingerprints. Students need access to a stamp pad, soap and water to wash their hands, and paper towels. You might provide one stamp pad for each pair, or set up several stations around the room with stamp pads.

■ Each student needs two 8½″ long paper strips, one to be used for their fingerprint picture and the other to be used to make their autograph book cover for the activity in Extensions For the Next Day. Make the strips by cutting 8½″ × 11″ sheets of paper into four equal strips.

■ Locate a copy of *Ed Emberley's Great Thumbprint Drawing Book* (Boston and Toronto: Little, Brown and Company, 1977). If you are unable to obtain this book, see the blackline master for directions on how to make fingerprints using a stamp pad and an example of how to make pictures with the fingerprints.

■ After the lesson, make one copy of each fingerprint strip for each student in the class. Four pictures can be copied on one 8½″ × 11″ sheet of paper and then cut apart.

Notes

Teacher

Help students review their work in this unit by asking questions, such as:

Q. By what numbers can you group and count?

Q. What number patterns did you discover when you counted by [2s], [5s], and [10s]?

Q. What have you learned about working cooperatively with a partner?

Introduce the activity by asking questions, such as:

Q. What is an autograph book?

Q. Why do people collect autographs?

Explain that students will make an autograph book to help them remember their partners and their classmates. Explain that students will make their autograph books with pages of their classmates' fingerprints.

Students

•• ••

•• ••

Notes	Teacher	Students

Teacher

Share and discuss *Ed Emberley's Great Thumbprint Drawing Book*. Model how to use a stamp pad to make fingerprints using all ten fingers. Use a thin-tip marker to make pictures with your fingerprints. Encourage students to offer suggestions. Model how to draw several different pictures.

Explain that students will stamp all ten of their fingerprints on strips of paper, make pictures with their fingerprints, and sign their paper strips. Explain that you will copy each student's fingerprint strip for everyone in the class and that in another class period you will distribute the pictures so that everyone has a copy of all the fingerprint pictures to make an autograph book.

Social Emphasis
Develop appropriate group skills.

Facilitate a discussion about how pairs might help each other make their fingerprints, how students might share the materials in a responsible way, and how students might help with clean-up procedures.

Students

•• ••
•• ••

Social Emphasis
Analyze the effect of behavior on others and on the group work.

Observe groups working and, when appropriate, ask questions, such as:

Q. **How are you helping each other with this activity? How is this affecting your work?**

Q. **How are you sharing the materials? How is this affecting your work?**

Q. **What picture are you making with your fingerprints?**

•• In pairs, students

1. Help each other stamp all of their fingerprints on a paper strip.

2. Make pictures with their fingerprints.

Notes	Teacher	Students

Mathematical Emphasis

Quantities of objects and sets of data can be grouped and counted in various ways.

A cooperative structure such as "Turn to Your Partner" (see p. xii) provides opportunities for all students to be involved in the discussion.

Collect the fingerprint pictures from each student and ask:

Q. **How many fingerprints are there on each strip of paper?**

Hold up two strips and ask questions, such as:

Q. **How many fingerprints are printed on these two strips all together? How do you know?**

Hold up five strips and ask questions, such as:

Q. **How many fingerprints are printed on these five strips all together? How do you know?**

Q. **What if I take away three strips, how many fingerprints will be left? How do you know?**

Continue holding up strips of fingerprints and asking similar questions.

Ask pairs to determine how many fingerprints will be in one autograph book. (You may wish to remind students that their autograph books will include ten fingerprints for each student in the class.)

•• ••

•• ••

Students may choose to use calculators, mental computation, or paper and pencil to solve this problem.

Observe pairs working and, when appropriate, ask questions, such as:

Q. **How are you working together to solve this problem?**

Q. **What information do you need to solve this problem?**

••

In pairs, students determine how many fingerprints will be in one autograph book.

| Notes | Teacher | Students |

Mathematical Emphasis

Operations can be carried out in a variety of ways.

Some pairs might solve the problem by counting by 10s. Other pairs might use their calculator to add ten 32 times or to multiply 10 times 32. Still others might use paper and pencil or a combination of strategies.

Have several pairs share the strategy they used to find the number of finger-prints in one autograph book. Ask questions, such as:

Q. How did you and your partner solve this problem? Did any pair use a different strategy? Explain.

Help students reflect on how they worked with their partner during the unit. Ask questions, such as:

Q. What did you like about the way you and your partner worked?

Q. What caused problems? How did you resolve them? How did you handle disagreements?

Q. How might you work differently the next time you work with a partner?

If appropriate, share some of your obser-vations of the differences between how pairs worked together at the beginning of the unit and how they work together now.

Give pairs an opportunity to thank each other and to share with each other what they liked about working together.

•• ••

•• ••

Extensions

For Pairs That Finish Early

■ Have partners help each other trace their hands on a sheet of drawing paper. Then, have students create a picture using their hand shapes.

For the Next Day

■ Distribute the pages of the fingerprint pictures to students. Have students staple the pages and their covers together to make their autograph books. Provide time for students to collect each other's autographs.

Directions for Making Fingerprint Pictures *

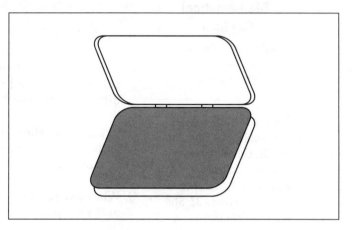

Use a damp, inky stamp pad.

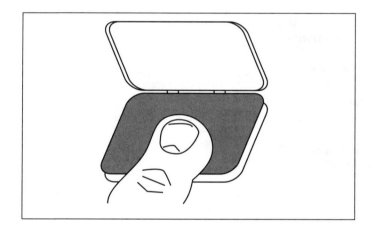

Press your thumb on the pad.

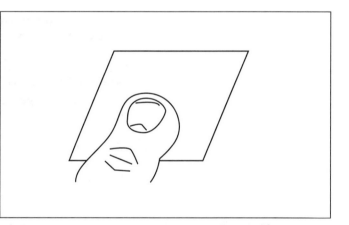

Press your thumb on the paper.

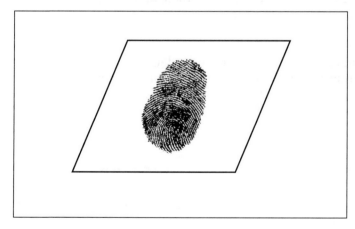

Let the print dry.

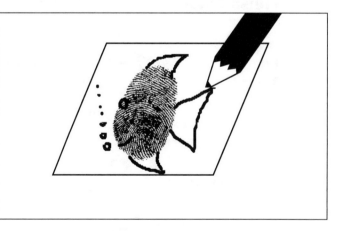

Then decorate it.

* Adapted from *Ed Emberley's Great Thumbprint Drawing Book* by Ed Emberley. (Boston and Toronto: Little, Brown and Company, 1977.)

Exploring Tens and Hundreds

Mathematical Development ■■■■■■

The focus of this unit is to foster students' understanding of place value concepts and of operations. Students continue to construct their understanding of these concepts as they group and count by 10s and 100s and compute with multiples of these numbers. The unit also provides opportunities for students to explore the relative magnitude of numbers and number patterns, to informally measure distance and capacity, and to experience some informal graphing.

Social Development ■■■■■■■

This unit builds on students' previous experience working with a partner and helps them continue to develop group skills, such as sharing materials, sharing the work, using materials responsibly, and explaining their thinking. Open-ended questions encourage students to examine how the underlying values of fairness, caring, and responsibility relate to behavior, and how their behavior affects their work and interaction. Students have many opportunities to reflect on and discuss ways to work effectively and to solve problems.

During the first lesson, pairs are formed randomly and stay together for the entire unit.

Mathematical Emphasis ■■■■■■

Conceptually, experiences in this unit help students construct their understanding that

- Our place value system is based on an organizational structure of grouping and regrouping.

- Numbers can be composed and decomposed.

- The relative magnitude of numbers can be described.

- A known quantity can be compared to an unknown quantity in order to make a reasonable estimate.

- Making a reasonable estimate requires gathering and using information.

- Operations can be carried out in a variety of ways.

- Measurement is approximate. Objects can be measured by making direct comparisons.

- Questions about our world can be asked, and data about those questions can be collected, organized, and analyzed.

- Classifying and sorting require the identification of specific attributes.

- Once a rule to generate a pattern has been identified, the pattern can usually be extended.

Social Emphasis ■■■■■■■

Socially, experiences in this unit help students to

- Develop appropriate group skills.

- Relate the values of fairness, caring, and responsibility to behavior.

- Analyze the effect of behavior on others and on the group work.

- Analyze why it is important to be fair, caring, and responsible.

- Take responsibility for learning and behavior.

Lessons

This unit includes nine lessons, plus an ongoing bulletin board activity. The calendar icon indicates that some preparation is needed or that an experience is suggested for the students prior to that lesson.

1. Tens, Anyone?
(page 65)

Team-building lesson that provides opportunities for students to count by 10s.

2. Beans and Stuff
(page 71)

Grouping lesson in which pairs estimate, group, and count objects by 10s and 1s.

3. Count by Tens
(page 77)

Calculator lesson in which pairs count by 10s and explore number patterns.

4. Place the Number
(page 83)

Spinner activity in which pairs find sums and determine their relative magnitudes.

5. Lima Beans 1
(page 93)

Grouping lesson in which pairs estimate, group, and count objects by 100s, 10s, and 1s.

6. Lima Beans 2
(page 99)

Measurement lesson in which pairs compare different-size containers, and estimate, group, and count objects by 100s, 10s, and 1s.

7. Paper Airplanes 1
(page 103)

Measurement lesson in which pairs use plastic chain links to measure, group, and count objects by 100s, 10s, and 1s.

8. Paper Airplanes 2
(page 109)

Data analysis lesson in which pairs collect, organize, and discuss data.

9. Where Does It Go?
(page 115)

Transition lesson in which pairs reflect on their work together and determine the relative magnitudes of numbers.

"Number of the Week" Bulletin Board

This ongoing activity provides opportunities for students to explore the relative magnitude and multiple meanings of a given number. At the beginning of each week, post a numeral and true/false statements about the number on a bulletin board. For example, you might post the number 68 and such statements as: "68 is about the number of students in our school." "68 is about the number of days in two months." "68 is closer to 50 than 100." "68 is about half of 140." Have pairs discuss each statement and decide whether they think it is true or false. Ask pairs to record their thinking and reasoning about each statement. At the end of the week, have students discuss the statements and their reasoning about each. Ask pairs to write a true statement of their own about the number and to share their statements with the class. Check for agreement or disagreement on the part of the class.

Materials

The materials needed for the unit are listed below. The first page of each lesson lists the materials specific to that lesson. Blackline masters for transparencies and group record sheets are included at the end of each lesson. Transparencies and other materials are available in the *Number Power* Package for Grade 2.

Throughout the unit, you will need access to an overhead projector, and students will need access to supplies such as calculators, scissors, crayons, rulers, glue sticks, paper, and pencils. The calculators students use in this unit should have the constant feature and should all be the same type. (While it is important that calculators be available at all times, they are listed on the first page of the lessons for which they are particularly important.) If possible, each group should have a container with all of these supplies available to use at their discretion.

Teacher Materials

- 2 sets of tens cards (Lesson 1)
- Transparencies of tens cards (Lesson 1)
- Baby food jar with 50 beans (Lesson 2)
- 16 baby food jars, filled (Lesson 2)
- Overhead calculator or transparency of a calculator (Lesson 3)
- Transparency of a Hundred Chart (Lesson 3)
- Transparency of "Count by Tens" direction sheet (Lesson 3)
- Transparency of "Place the Number" group record sheet (Lesson 4)
- 2 overhead spinners (Lesson 4)
- 8-oz. cup with beans (Lessons 5 and 6)
- Empty container with capacity other than 8-oz. (Lesson 6)
- "How Far Did Your Airplane Fly?" graph (Lesson 8)
- Transparency of "Where Does It Go?" group record sheet (Lesson 9)

Student Materials

Each student needs

- Construction paper to make a folder

Each pair needs

- 8½″ x 11″ sheet of tagboard (Lesson 1)
- Baby food jar with beans (Lesson 2)
- Calculator with constant feature (Lessons 2 and 3)
- Hundred Chart (Lessons 3, 4, and 9)

- "Place the Number" group record sheet (Lesson 4)
- 2 spinners (Lesson 4)
- 8-oz. cup with beans (Lesson 5)
- Twenty to thirty 3-oz. paper cups (Lessons 5 and 6)
- Two or three 16-oz. margarine tubs (Lessons 5 and 6)
- Self-stick notes (Lessons 5 and 6)
- Two-Hundred Chart (Lessons 5 and 9)
- 8-oz. plastic cup (Lesson 6)
- 4 containers of different capacities (Lesson 6)
- Baggie with beans (Lesson 6)
- About 200 plastic chain links (Lessons 7 and 8)
- String (Lessons 7 and 8)
- Paper clip (Lesson 7)
- "Where Does It Go?" group record sheet (Lesson 9)

Extension Materials

- *From One to One Hundred* by Teri Sloat (New York: Dutton Children's Books, a division of Penguin Books, 1991) (Lesson 1)
- Four 8½″ x 11″ signs (Lesson 4)

Each pair needs

- Hundred Chart (Lessons 1 and 4)
- Baggies with counters (Lesson 2)
- Calculator with constant feature (Lessons 3 and 6)
- Two-Hundred Chart (Lesson 3)
- Number card (Lesson 4)

Teaching Hints

- Several of the lessons require the use of different-size containers (see Lessons 2, 5, and 6). It might be helpful to start collecting the containers at the beginning of the unit.

- Prior to each lesson, think about open-ended questions you might ask to extend and probe the thinking of your students. Decide which Extensions to have ready when pairs finish early.

- Provide time for students to freely explore unfamiliar or infrequently used materials before each lesson.

- In Lesson 1, students are asked to select a name for their pair. If students have not had experience creating names, you might wish to suggest a theme for the pair names, such as a name that includes a shape (for example, the Terrific Triangles or the Radical Rectangles), a name that reflects the season (such as the Winter Wonders or the Super Snowballs), or a name made from parts of their individual names. Have pairs develop a table sign with their pair name to be displayed in their work area when they work as a pair. Frequently refer to the pairs using their pair names.

- Some questions are suggested at the end of Lessons 2, 6, and 8 that may take students a considerable amount of time to explore. For example, in Lesson 6, students are asked to determine the difference between the number of beans that containers of different capacities hold. You will need to extend the length of these lessons or have students investigate these questions during other class periods.

- Have calculators available at all times during this unit for students to use when they choose. Throughout the unit, ask if any students have used calculators for their work and lead an informal discussion about their use.

- Encourage students to organize their counting so that they can look at the objects and count them easily. For example, students might group objects on a sheet of paper and circle each group, or they might count objects into paper cups.

- After each lesson, review any Extensions that students have not explored and decide whether to have students investigate these Extensions before going on to the next lesson.

Assessment Techniques

These informal assessment techniques will help you assess students' understanding of grouping by 10s and their ability to make reasonable estimates. These techniques are not intended to determine mastery. Students' understanding will vary from experience to experience, particularly as they are beginning to construct their understanding.

Use the following assessment techniques throughout this unit and when indicated in a particular lesson. As you observe, note students' conceptual understanding as well as their behavior (for example, some students might exhibit confidence, while others may give up easily). Prepare possible questions ahead of time. Be open to and allow time for students' responses, and probe their thinking by asking follow-up questions that require them to explain further. Whenever possible, record students' responses. Compare students' responses over time to assess growth in their conceptual understanding.

Observe Individual Students Estimating, Grouping, and Counting

As students work, observe individuals and ask yourself questions, such as:

> Q. Does the student use referents (such as the teacher's baby food jar containing exactly 50 beans in Lesson 2) to estimate, or does the student simply guess? Is the estimate reasonable?

If a student chooses not to use the referent, do not force the issue. Students will need many experiences estimating as they construct an understanding of the logic of using a referent to make a reasonable estimate.

> Q. Does the student group and count by 10s, or does the student ignore the groups of 10 and count each object one by one? Does the student count the extra objects by 1s if there are not enough to make a 10?

Some students may continue to count the extra objects by 10s. Some students may count the objects by 1s even though they are grouped into sets of 10. All of these students will need more experiences grouping and counting objects by 10s. Students construct an understanding of grouping over time.

> Q. Does the student regroup ten sets of 10 to one set of 100? If there are not enough to make another 100, does the student count the remaining objects by 10s and 1s ?

Some students may not regroup ten sets of 10 to 100. Some students may count the extra 1s as 10s or 100s. All of these students will need more experiences grouping and regrouping objects to and past 100. Students will construct an understanding of grouping and regrouping over time.

Assess Individual Students' Ability to Group by 10s

- Display 85 sticks. Ask, "How many do you think there are? Can you group them by 10s? How many 10s? Are any left over? How many do you think you have? How can you be sure? Can you count them any other way? Show me."

- Display 53 buttons. Ask the student to count the buttons by 10s. If the student is able to count by 10s, ask, "How many are there? What if I separate one group of 10 and make five smaller groups?" (Break apart one group of 10 into five groups of 2. Leave the other groups of 10 intact.) Ask, "How many buttons are there on the table now?"

- Display 36 sticks bundled into three sets of 10, with 6 sticks left over. Have the student count the sticks. Ask, "How many sticks are there? If I put out some more sticks (add 5 more sticks to the 36 sticks already out), how many are there now?" Notice how the student deals with the additional sticks.

- Display 115 straws. Ask, "How many do you think there are?" Have the student group the straws by 10 and count them. Ask, "How many do you have? How many 10s? How many 100s? Are there any left over? After we group by 10s, what do you do when you reach 100 objects?"

Student Writing

Throughout the unit, ask students to verbalize their thinking, and at times to explain their thinking in writing. During this unit, students are asked frequently to write statements about numbers. These statements will be used in the last lesson of the unit, "Where Does It Go?"

Tens, Anyone?

Students take turns discussing their favorite things, then choose a pair name and make a table sign. Students count by tens and mentally add tens to multiples of ten.

Team Builder Emphasis

In this lesson, students

- Count by 10s.
- Get to know each other.
- Develop a sense of identity.
- Begin to develop an effective working relationship.

Students add to their understanding that

- Our place value system is based on an organizational structure of grouping and regrouping.

Social Emphasis

In this lesson, students

- Listen to others.
- Share the work.

Students continue to

- Develop appropriate group skills.
- Analyze the effect of behavior on others and on the group work.

Group Size: 2

Teacher Materials

- 2 sets of tens cards (see Before the Lesson)
- Transparencies of tens cards (see Before the Lesson)

Student Materials

Each pair needs

- 8½″ × 11″ sheet of tagboard
- Crayons or markers

Extension Materials

- *From One to One Hundred* (see Extensions)

Each pair needs

- Access to a Hundred Chart (see Unit 1, Lesson 8)
- Crayons or markers

If we take away 20, how many will we have left?

- Copy two sets of tens cards using the blackline masters and cut apart. Use these cards in the beginning of the lesson to group students.

- Make transparencies of the 2 tens cards blackline masters and cut apart. Use these transparencies at the end of the lesson to help students count by 10s and add sets of 10.

Notes	Teacher	Students
	Randomly group students by distributing the tens cards and asking students to find the person with the identical card. Explain that these pairs will work together during this unit as the class explores grouping and counting by 10s. Introduce the lesson and explain that in order to get to know each other better, partners will take turns telling each other five of their favorite things. Model by sharing five of your favorite things. As a class, brainstorm ideas of favorite things to discuss, such as their favorite food, toy, or song.	●● ●● ●● ●●
	Observe pairs as they discuss their favorite things and ask questions, such as: **Q. What is one of your partner's favorite things?** **Q. Do you have any of the same favorite things? What are they?**	●● In pairs, students tell each other five of their favorite things.
	Have several students tell the class one of their partner's favorite things. Ask if any other students had also discussed these favorites. Explain that pairs are to choose a name for their pair and make a table sign to use each time they work together. Model how to make the table sign by folding the tagboard in half lengthwise. Ask pairs to write their pair name on the table sign and draw the 10 favorite things they discussed. (If both students have a favorite in common, such as pizza, they should draw that favorite twice.)	●● ●● ●● ●●

Notes	Teacher	Students

Social Emphasis
Develop appropriate group skills.

Facilitate a discussion about how students might work together. Ask questions, such as:

Q. What have you learned about working with a partner?

Q. What might you and your partner do that will help you work well together?

•• ••
•• ••

If students are having difficulty working together, ask questions, such as:

Q. What seems to be causing problems? What might you do to change this?

Q. What have you tried? What else could you try? How might that help?

As pairs work, ask questions, such as:

Q. How did you choose the name for your pair?

Q. How are you sharing the work? Are you both happy with this? Why?

•• In pairs, students

1. Choose a name for their pair.

2. Make a table sign showing their pair name and their 10 favorite things.

Mathematical Emphasis
Our place value system is based on an organizational structure of grouping and regrouping.

A cooperative structure such as "Turn to Your Partner" (see p. xii) can provide opportunities for all students to reflect on a problem and discuss their thinking.

Have pairs introduce themselves and share their table signs with the class. Ask questions, such as:

Q. What are some favorite things pairs have in common?

Q. How might we count all the favorite things on 10 table signs? Is there another way? Let's try it.

Q. How might we count all the favorite things on all of the table sign? How do you know? Let's try it.

•• ••
•• ••

Place one of the tens card transparencies on the overhead, and ask:

•• ••

•• ••

Q. How many objects do you see? (10)

Add another tens card transparency, and ask:

Q. How many objects now? (20) **How do you know?**

Add two more transparencies, and ask:

Q. How many objects now? (40) **How do you know?**

Q. There are 40 objects. If we take away 10 objects (remove a tens card transparency), **how many objects are there?** (30) **How do you know?**

Continue adding and removing transparencies and asking similar questions.

Help students reflect on the lesson by asking questions, such as:

Q. What did you like about the way you and your partner worked together?

Q. What helped you work together? What could you do next time that might help you work together better?

Social Emphasis

Analyze the effect of behavior on others and on the group work.

Extensions

For Pairs That Finish Early

■ Have students take turns counting to 100, first by 1s and then by 10s. Students might need to use a Hundred Chart (see Unit 1, Lesson 8) to help them count.

For the Next Day

■ Read aloud and discuss the book *From One to One Hundred* by Teri Sloat (New York: Dutton Children's Books, a division of Penguin Books, 1991). Discuss the pictures and have pairs make an accordion book with 10 pages, each page showing a set of 10 objects, people, or animals. Have students show the cumulative total by numbering the pages starting with 10. For example:

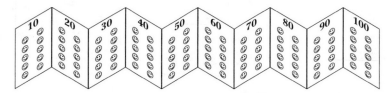

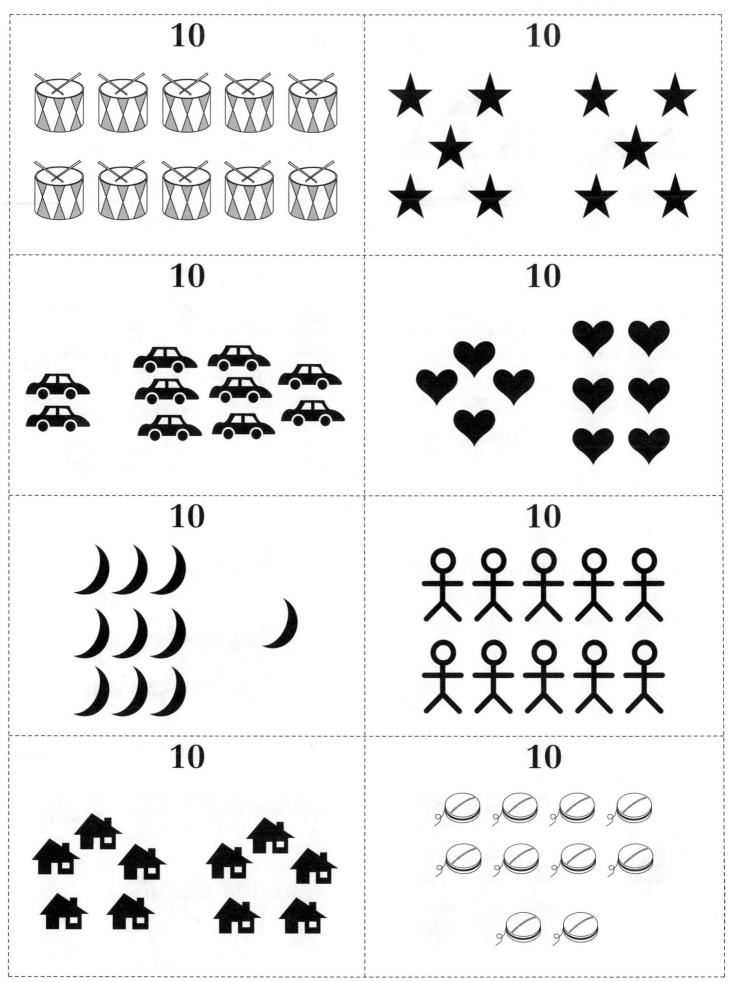

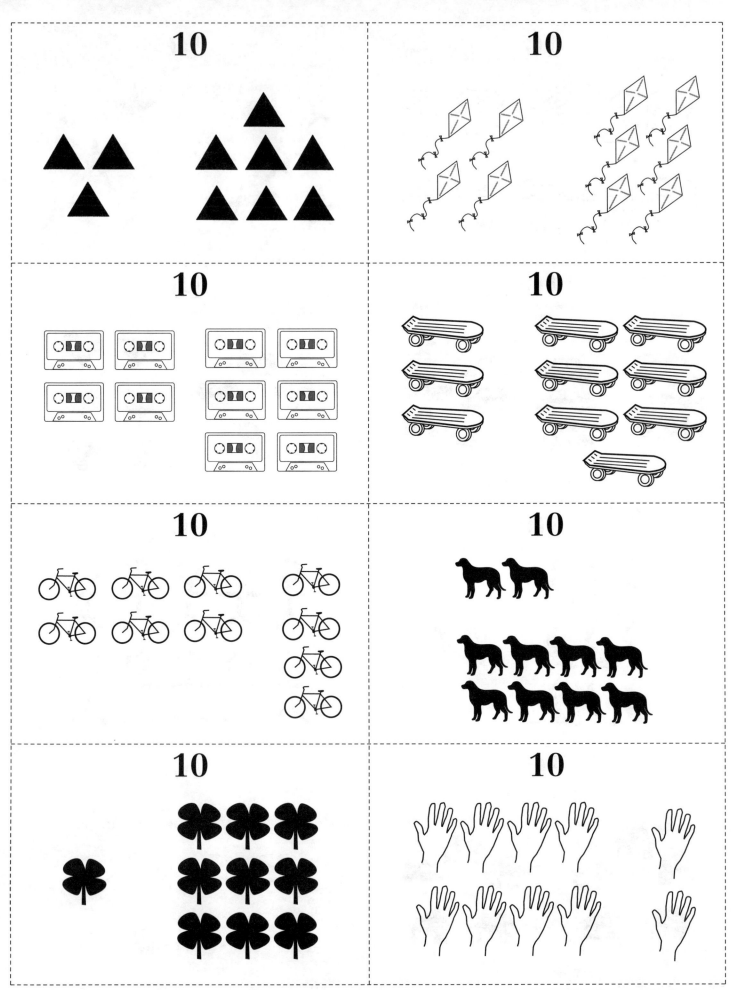

Beans and Stuff

Students estimate, group, count, and record the number of objects in jars. This lesson may take more than one class period.

DAYS AHEAD
1

Mathematical Emphasis

In this lesson, students

- Make an estimate.
- Group and count by 10s and 1s.
- Compute informally.

Students add to their understanding that

- A known quantity can be compared to an unknown quantity in order to make a reasonable estimate.
- Our place value system is based on an organizational structure of grouping and regrouping.
- Operations can be carried out in a variety of ways.

Social Emphasis

In this lesson, students

- Use materials responsibly.
- Share the work.
- Help each other.

Students continue to

- Develop appropriate group skills.
- Relate the values of fairness, caring, and responsibility to behavior.
- Analyze the effect of behavior on others and on the group work.

Group Size: 2

Teacher Materials

- Baby food jar with 50 beans (see Before the Lesson)
- 16 baby food jars, filled (see Before the Lesson)

Student Materials

Each student needs

- Construction paper to make a folder

Each pair needs

- Baby food jar with 100 beans (see Before the Lesson)
- Access to a calculator

Extension Materials

Each pair needs

- Baggies with counters (see Before the Lesson)

DAYS AHEAD

1

- For each pair, put slightly fewer than 100 kidney or pinto beans in a baby food jar. Vary how many beans are in each jar. Use one of these jars to introduce the lesson.

- For use as a referent, put exactly 50 kidney or pinto beans in a baby food jar. (Use the same type of beans for both this jar and the pairs' jars.)

- Fill 16 baby food jars: 4 with dry pasta (such as elbow macaroni), 4 with lima beans, 4 with small counters, and 4 with pebbles. If these materials are not available, substitute other small objects. Place these jars in a central location. (Each jar should contain fewer than 100 objects.)

- Fill about 30 baggies, each with fewer than 100 counters. Vary the number and type of counters in each baggie.

Notes	Teacher	Students

Explain that during this unit students will have many opportunities to estimate and count numbers of objects, and to write about these numbers. Ask students to make a folder for their writing by folding their construction paper in half and writing their names on it. Ask students to title a sheet of writing paper "Beans and Stuff."

Show one of the students' bean-filled jars and have students discuss:

Q. About how many beans do you think are in this jar?

Show the referent jar, and explain that it contains 50 beans. Ask students again to discuss:

Q. About how many beans do you think are in your jar?

Have pairs estimate the number of beans in their jars and individually record this estimate on their "Beans and Stuff" record sheet. Ask pairs to report their estimates, and list these where all can see. Ask questions, such as:

Q. What is the lowest estimate in the class? The highest?

Mathematical Emphasis

A known quantity can be compared to an unknown quantity in order to make a reasonable estimate.

Notes	Teacher	Students
	Q. **Look at the lowest and highest estimates. Where does your estimate fit? Near the lowest estimate? The highest estimate? In the middle? How do you know?**	•• •• •• ••
Social Emphasis Relate the values of fairness, caring, and responsibility to behavior.	Explain that pairs will group and count their beans by 10s and then individually record the actual number of beans in their jar. Facilitate a discussion about how students might use the materials responsibly and share the work.	
Observe how partners interact. Note positive interaction and any problems you might discuss as the class reflects on the lesson.	**O**bserve pairs working and, when appropriate, ask questions, such as: Q. **How are you sharing the work? Is that fair? Do you both agree?** Q. **If you counted your beans by 5s, how many groups of 5 would you have? How do you know?**	•• In pairs, students 1. Group and count the beans in their jars by 10s. 2. Individually record the actual number of beans in their jars on their "Beans and Stuff" record sheets.
	Have pairs report the actual number of beans in their jars, and record these numbers where all can see. Ask questions, such as: Q. **What is the fewest number of beans? The greatest number of beans?** Q. **Were the class estimates reasonable? Why?** Have pairs set aside their jars of beans. Have one member of each pair select one of the 16 baby food jars that contains different objects. Explain that pairs are to repeat the process of estimating, recording, grouping and counting by 10s, and then comparing estimates and actual counts. Ask pairs to return their jars to the central location when they finish, then choose jars containing objects that they have not counted and repeat the process a third time.	•• •• •• ••

Notes	Teacher	Students

As you observe, ask yourself questions, such as:

Q. Do students count the groups by 10s, or do they ignore the group-ings and count each object individually?

Q. Can students add 10s and multiples of 10 up to 100?

Observe pairs working and ask ques-tions, such as:

Q. Count your objects. How many all together? How many sets of 10? How many objects would you have if you took away two 10s? If you added three 10s?

●● In pairs, students

1. Choose a new jar of objects and estimate how many objects are in the jar.

2. Individually record the estimate.

3. Group and count the objects by 10s and individually record the actual number of objects.

4. Repeat the process several times with baby food jars con-taining different sets of objects.

Mathematical Emphasis

Operations can be carried out in a variety of ways.

Have several pairs report their findings. First in pairs, and then as a class, discuss questions, such as:

●● ●●

●● ●●

Students may choose to use calculators, mental computation, paper and pencil, or a combination of these strategies to help them solve these problems.

Provide sufficient time for students to explore these questions.

You might wish to write a frame sentence as a model for students to use if they choose. For exam-ple:

The jar with the _____ had ___ _____ .

Students might write, "The jar with the <u>beans</u> had <u>98</u> <u>beans</u>."

Q. Compare your estimates with the actual number of objects in each jar. What do you notice?

Q. If I gave you a jar that was twice as large as the baby food jar and filled it with [pasta], about how many [pieces of pasta] would be in the jar? How do you know?

Q. What is the difference between the number of [pebbles] and the number of [counters]? How do you know?

Ask students to help each other write statements about the number of objects in each jar. Have several students suggest some possible statements. Explain that students will save these statements in their folders to use in the last lesson of the unit.

Notes	Teacher	Students

As you observe students, ask yourself questions, such as:

Q. Are students willing to help each other?

Q. What observations can I share with students about how I see them working together?

Observe students working and, when appropriate, ask questions, such as:

Q. What are you writing?

Q. How are you helping each other?

••

In pairs, students help each other write sentences about the number of objects in the jars.

Social Emphasis
Analyze the effect of behavior on others and on the group work.

As a class, reflect on the lesson. Ask questions, such as:

Q. How is this lesson similar to or different from previous lessons?

Q. What helped you work? What problems did you have? How did that make you feel? How did you resolve them?

Q. In what ways did you and your partner help each other? How did that make you feel?

Q. What can you say about how you and your partner shared the materials?

If appropriate, share some of your observations of the positive interaction and the problems you noted as pairs worked.

•• ••

•• ••

Extensions

For Pairs That Finish Early

■ Ask students to predict how many groups of 2 they would have if they grouped the [beans] by 2s. Have pairs check their prediction by grouping their [beans] by 2s.

For the Next Day

■ Give pairs baggies with different amounts and different types of counters prepared before the lesson. Ask them to estimate the number of counters in their baggies. Have students count the objects using any grouping other than counting by 1s.

■ Begin the "Number of the Week" bulletin board activity, described in the Overview, p. 60.

Count by Tens

Students count by tens using calculators and Hundred Charts and explore the resulting number patterns.

Mathematical Emphasis

In this lesson, students

- Count by 10s.
- Look for patterns.

Students add to their understanding that

- Once a rule to generate a pattern has been identified, the pattern can usually be extended.
- Our place value system is based on an organizational structure of grouping and regrouping.

Social Emphasis

In this lesson, students

- Explain their thinking.
- Share the work.
- Help each other.

Students continue to

- Develop appropriate group skills.
- Analyze why it is important to be fair, caring, and responsible.

Group Size: 2

Teacher Materials

- Overhead calculator or a transparency of a calculator similar to students' calculators
- Transparency of a Hundred Chart (see Unit 1, Lesson 8)
- Transparency of "Count by Tens" direction sheet

Student Materials

Each pair needs

- Calculator with a constant feature (all calculators should be the same type)
- Hundred Chart (see Unit 1, Lesson 8)

Extension Materials

Each pair needs

- Calculator
- Two-Hundred Chart

Introduce the lesson by facilitating a discussion about the mathematics that students have explored during this unit and the previous unit. Ask questions, such as:

Q. What mathematics have you explored in previous lessons?

Q. By what numbers can you group and count?

Q. What have you learned about the calculator?

Show the Hundred Chart transparency and ask students to count by 10s. As students count, point to the numbers on the Hundred Chart. Ask questions, such as:

Q What patterns do you notice when you count by 10s?

Explain that students will continue to explore number patterns on their calculators and Hundred Charts. Show the "Count by Tens" direction sheet transparency and explain that pairs will

- clear the calculator
- choose a number from 1 through 9
- press that number
- press +
- press 10 (to count by 10s)
- press = =
- find and circle on the Hundred Chart each number they see in the calculator window

Use an overhead calculator or a transparency of a calculator to show students which keys to press as you give directions. For example, clear the calculator, and enter 2. Circle 2 on the Hundred Chart. Press +, and enter 10, but do not circle 10 on the Hundred Chart. Press =; 12 should be displayed in the window of the calculator. Circle 12 on the Hundred Chart.

Demonstrate with the following example:

- clear the calculator
- press 2
- press +
- press 10
- press = = = = (and so on)

As you press =, demonstrate circling on the Hundred Chart transparency the number you see in the calculator window (2, 12, 22, 32, 42, etc.). Explain that students will circle the first number in the sequence and each following number, but not the counter 10.

Observe how partners interact. Note positive interaction and any problems you might discuss as the class reflects on the lesson.

Observe pairs working and, when appropriate, ask questions, such as:

Q. **What are you and your partner discovering?**

Q. **If you press = twice, what number do you think you will see in the calculator window? Why? Try it.**

Q. **How are you working together? Are you working in a way that is helping you both? How?**

●● In pairs, students

1. clear the calculator

2. choose and press any number from 1 through 9

3. press +

4. enter 10

5. press = =

6. circle the number on their Hundred Chart that they see in the calculator window each time they press =

Mathematical Emphasis

Once a rule to generate a pattern has been identified, the pattern can usually be extended.

Display several of the students' completed Hundred Charts where all can see. Ask questions, such as:

Q. **What patterns do you notice?**

Q. **Based on this pattern** (point to one of the Hundred Charts), **what number would come next in the sequence?** (Have students extend the pattern; for example, 84, 94, 104, 114, and so on.)

●● ●●

●● ●●

Social Emphasis

Analyze why it is important to be fair, caring, and responsible.

Help students reflect on their work with their partner by asking questions, such as:

Q. **What went well for you and your partner? What did you do that helped you work well together?**

Q. **How did you tell your partner what you were thinking?**

Q. **Why is it important to share your thinking with your partner?**

If appropriate, share some of your observations of the positive interaction and the problems you noted as pairs worked.

Notes	Teacher	Students

To help students develop their understanding of number patterns and grouping and counting by 10s past 100, have pairs investigate the activities in Extensions before going on to the next lesson.

Extensions

For Pairs That Finish Early

■ Have pairs play Find That Counter again. (One partner clears the calculator, enters a secret number from 1 through 9, presses +, then presses = =. The other partner takes the calculator and tries to guess the hidden counter by continuing to press = and looking at the numbers displayed in the calculator window.)

For the Next Day

■ Have pairs find number patterns on a Two-Hundred Chart. Explain that pairs will

- clear the calculator
- choose a number from 101 through 109
- press that number
- press +
- press 10 (to count by 10s)
- press = =
- find each number displayed in the calculator window and circle it on the Two-Hundred Chart. First in pairs, then as a class, discuss the resulting number patterns.

■ Continue with the "Number of the Week" bulletin board activity described in the Overview, p. 60.

Count by Tens
Directions

1. Clear the calculator $\boxed{C}$.

2. Choose and enter a number from 1 through 9.

3. Circle the number you entered on your Hundred Chart.

4. Press $\boxed{+}$.

5. Enter $\boxed{1}$ $\boxed{0}$.

6. Press $\boxed{=}$.

7. Circle the number you see in your calculator window on your Hundred Chart.

8. Press $\boxed{=}$.

9. Circle the number you see in your calculator window on your Hundred Chart.

10. Continue to press $\boxed{=}$ and circle the numbers you see in your calculator window on your Hundred Chart.

Two-Hundred Chart

101	102	103	104	105	106	107	108	109	110
111	112	113	114	115	116	117	118	119	120
121	122	123	124	125	126	127	128	129	130
131	132	133	134	135	136	137	138	139	140
141	142	143	144	145	146	147	148	149	150
151	152	153	154	155	156	157	158	159	160
161	162	163	164	165	166	167	168	169	170
171	172	173	174	175	176	177	178	179	180
181	182	183	184	185	186	187	188	189	190
191	192	193	194	195	196	197	198	199	200

Place the Number

Students spin two spinners, find the sum of the numbers generated by the spinners, and determine the relative magnitude of the sum. This lesson may take more than one class period.

DAYS AHEAD 1

Mathematical Emphasis

In this lesson, students

- Add 10s and 1s.
- Determine the relative magnitude of numbers.

Students add to their understanding that

- The relative magnitude of numbers can be described.

Social Emphasis

In this lesson, students

- Agree on solutions.
- Share the work.
- Explain their thinking.

Students continue to

- Develop appropriate group skills.
- Relate the values of fairness, caring, and responsibility to behavior.

Group Size: 2

Teacher Materials

- Transparency of "Place the Number" group record sheet
- 2 overhead spinners (see Before the Lesson)

Student Materials

Each pair needs

- "Place the Number" group record sheet
- 2 spinners (see Before the Lesson)
- Access to a Hundred Chart (see Unit 1, Lesson 8)

Extension Materials

- Four 8½″ × 11″ signs (see Before the Lesson)

Each pair needs

- Number card (see Before the Lesson)
- Access to a Hundred Chart (see Unit 1, Lesson 8)

- Make 2 spinners for each pair and 2 overhead spinners for yourself using the blackline masters (see "Directions for Making Spinners" for instructions). One spinner will have a face labeled 0–9 and one spinner will have a face labeled 10–60. It is helpful if the students' spinner labeled 0–9 is a different color from the student spinner labeled 10–60.

- For Extensions, prepare a number card for each pair by copying the number card blackline master and cutting on the dotted lines.

- Also for Extensions, make four 8½″ × 11″ signs labeled as follows: Closer to 25; Closer to 50; Closer to 75; Closer to 100.

Notes

Students may need to use a Hundred Chart to help them determine the relative magnitude of the numbers discussed.

You might want to discuss such things as sharing the spinning of the spinners, together adding the two numbers indicated by the spinners, listening and sharing ideas about where to place the sum, and agreeing in which box to place the sum.

Teacher

Introduce the lesson by showing the spinners and explaining that pairs will play a game in which they decide whether a number is closer to one number than another.

Explain that students will spin the spinners and add the two numbers generated by the spinners. Model this by spinning the two overhead spinners and having students add the numbers. Show the "Place the Number" transparency and have pairs decide in which box to write the sum. Explain that some of the sums will belong in more than one box (for example, 61) and that students would write those sums in more than one box. The "Numbers that do not fit" box on the group record sheet has been provided to accommodate sums that do not fit in the other boxes. For example, 41 will go in the "Numbers that do not fit" box.

With a student, model playing the game and working cooperatively with your partner. As a class, discuss what you and your partner did that helped you work well together.

Students

•• ••

•• ••

As you observe students working, ask yourself questions, such as:

Q. How are students handling differences of opinion?

Q. How are students finding the sums?

Q. How are students handling such numbers as 45 and 50?

Q. Do students have a sense of the magnitude of a number in relation to other numbers?

If students have trouble cooperating with each other, help them analyze the situation by posing open-ended questions, such as:

Q. What seems to be causing problems?

Q. What could you do about that?

Q. How might that help?

Observe pairs working. Ask questions, such as:

Q. How are you finding the sums?

Q. Where would you place the number 20? Why?

Q. Have you placed a number in the "Numbers that do not fit" box? Why?

Q. Have you put any numbers in more than one box? Which numbers? Why did you decide they belong in these boxes?

Q. How are you sharing the work? Is that helping you and your partner work?

Q. How are you explaining your thinking? Why is that important?

Q. How are you making sure you both agree on a solution?

•• In pairs, students

1. Spin the two spinners and find the sum of the two numbers generated.

2. Decide in which box the sum belongs.

3. Record on the group record sheet and prepare to share their thinking.

Mathematical Emphasis

The relative magnitude of numbers can be described.

Encourage students to explain their thinking.

Students may place the same number in different boxes. Accept any placements that students can justify and use this situation to extend students' thinking about the relative magnitude of numbers.

Show the "Place the Number" transparency. Have several pairs share one of their sums and the box in which they placed the sum. Check for agreement on the part of the class. Ask students to explain why they agree or disagree. Ask questions, such as:

Q. Could that sum fit in another box? Explain.

Q. Where could a sum of [50] be placed? Why?

Q. Where could a sum of [45] be placed? Why?

Q. How did you decide which numbers to put in the "Numbers that do not fit" box?

•• ••

•• ••

Notes	**Teacher**	**Students**

Q. How is this lesson similar to or different from previous lessons?

•• ••

•• ••

Q. What did you learn from playing this game?

Help students reflect on their work together. Facilitate a discussion about responsibility and ask questions, such as:

Social Emphasis

Relate the values of fairness, caring, and responsibility to behavior.

Q. What does it mean to act responsibly or to take responsibility?

Q. How did you and your partner act responsibly?

Q. What problems did you and your partner have? How might you avoid those problems next time?

To help students develop an understanding of the relative magnitude of numbers, have pairs investigate the activities in Extensions before going on to the next lesson.

Extensions

For Pairs That Finish Early

- Have pairs make up their own boxes for sorting the numbers, such as "more than 50/less than 50," or "closer to 50 than to 100/closer to 100 than to 50" and have pairs re-sort their numbers.

For the Next Day

- In the four corners of the room, hang signs labeled as follows: Closer to 25; Closer to 50; Closer to 75; Closer to 100.

  Distribute a number card to each pair (see Before the Lesson). Ask pairs to read the numeral and decide in which of the four corners their card belongs and then stand in that corner of the room. (Pairs might need to use a Hundred Chart to help them determine the relative magnitude of their numbers.) Ask pairs to share with the class why they think their number is closer to 25, 50, 75, or 100.

Place the Number
Directions

Spin the two spinners, add the two numbers, and decide in which box to write the sum. Some of the sums can be written in more than one box.

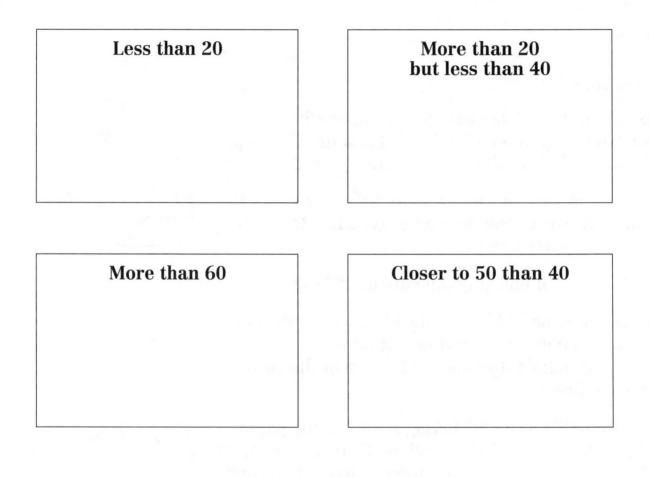

Less than 20

More than 20
but less than 40

More than 60

Closer to 50 than 40

Numbers that do not fit

Directions for Making Spinners*

Materials for one spinner

- Spinner face (copy blackline master and cut; copy on a transparency for the overhead spinners)
- 3″ × 5″ index card
- 3/8″ piece of a drinking straw
- paper clip or a bobby pin
- ruler
- tape

Instructions

1. Bend up the outside part of the paper clip as shown (or open up a bobby pin) and use the point to poke a hole in the center of the spinner face.

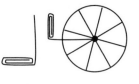

2. Poke a hole in the center of an index card with the paper clip or bobby pin and draw a line from the center to one corner.

3. Cut a piece of masking tape about 2″ long.

4. Poke the paper clip or bobby pin through the center of the index card and tape it on the bottom of the card to hold it in place. (The top of the card has the line.)

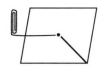

5. Put the 3/8″ piece of drinking straw on the paper clip or bobby pin that is sticking through the top of the card. It will serve as a washer to keep the spinner face off the index card.

6. Put the spinner face on next.

7. Cover the point of the paper clip with a piece of tape to keep the spinner from spinning off (this step can be omitted if using a bobby pin).

tape

* Adapted from *The Math Solution* by Marilyn Burns. (Sausalito, CA: The Math Solution Publications, 1991.)

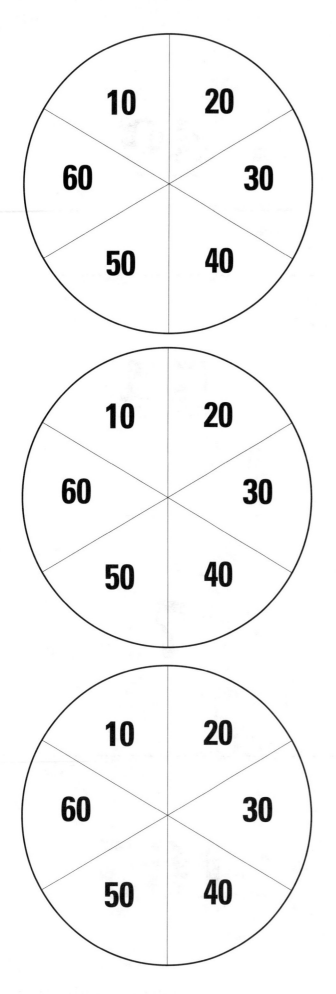
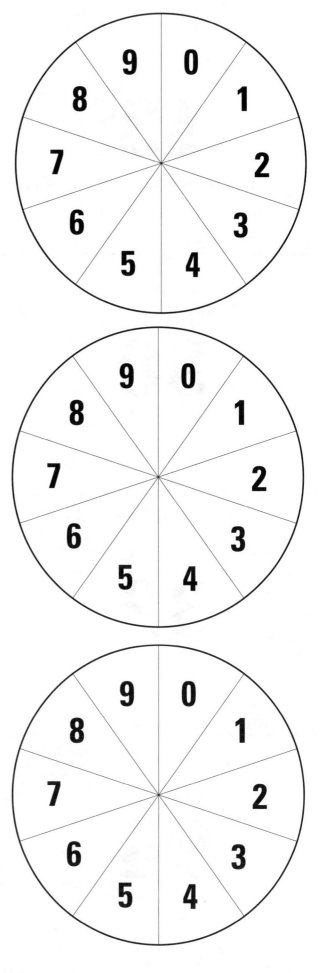

13	49
80	54
32	7
94	105

23	**46**
78	**61**
28	**21**
99	**72**

Lima Beans 1

Students use a referent to help them estimate the number of lima beans in a container. They then group and count the beans by hundreds, tens, and ones, and compare their estimate with the actual number.

DAYS AHEAD
3

Mathematical Emphasis

In this lesson, students

- Make an estimate.
- Group and count by 100s, 10s, and 1s.

Students add to their understanding that

- Making a reasonable estimate requires gathering and using information.
- Our place value system is based on an organizational structure of grouping and regrouping.

Social Emphasis

In this lesson, students

- Share the work.
- Use materials responsibly.

Students continue to

- Develop appropriate group skills.
- Analyze the effect of behavior on others and on the group work.

Group Size: 2

Teacher Materials

- 8-oz. cup with about 80 beans (see Before the Lesson)

Student Materials

Each pair needs

- 8-oz. cup filled with beans (see Before the Lesson)
- Twenty to thirty 3-oz. paper cups for grouping sets of 10 beans
- Two or three 16-oz. margarine tubs for grouping sets of 100 beans
- 2 self-stick notes
- Two-Hundred Chart (see Lesson 3)

Each student needs

- Folder (from Lesson 2)

DAYS AHEAD 3

■ Put approximately 80 large lima beans in an 8-oz. clear plastic cup to introduce the lesson.

■ For each pair, fill one 8-oz. clear plastic cup to the brim with large lima beans. Use large beans, so the number is manageable for counting. The cup will hold approximately 180 to 210 large beans.

■ This lesson is the first experience in the *Number Power* program in which students group and count numbers of objects greater than 100. If students have had little experience counting more than 100 objects, provide several opportunities for them to do so prior to this lesson.

Notes	Teacher	Students
	Introduce the lesson by showing the 8-oz. cup containing approximately 80 lima beans. Ask students to predict whether there are more or fewer than 100 beans in the cup. Discuss students' predictions, and then explain that you put about 80 lima beans in the cup.	•• •• •• ••
	Explain that each pair will estimate the number of lima beans in their cup, write their estimate on a self-stick note, and place their self-stick note where all can see.	
	Facilitate a discussion about how students might use the materials responsibly and how they might share the work.	

As you observe, ask yourself questions, such as:

Q. Do students use my cup of beans to help them estimate? If so, how?

Q. Do students have a sense of the reasonableness of their estimates? Some students may not be ready to make reasonable estimates and will need more experiences.

Observe pairs working and, when appropriate, ask questions, such as:

Q. How are you estimating the number of beans?

Q. How are you sharing the work?

•• In pairs, students

1. Estimate the number of beans in their cups.

2. Write their estimates on self-stick notes.

3. Place their self-stick notes where all can see.

Notes	Teacher	Students

Mathematical Emphasis

Making a reasonable estimate requires gathering and using information.

Ask students to help you arrange the self-stick notes in order from the lowest to the highest estimate. Ask questions, such as:

Q. Is your estimate closer to the lowest estimate, the highest, or in the middle of the estimates? How do you know?

Q. How did you estimate the number of beans in your cup?

•• ••

•• ••

Consider discussing the regrouping process. You might wish to ask questions, such as:

Q. If you have nine groups of 10 beans and you add one more group of 10 beans, how many beans do you have all together? [100] Show me.

Ask pairs to group and count the beans by 10s (using 3-oz. cups for grouping sets of 10 beans and 16-oz. margarine tubs for regrouping sets of 10 to 100). Have pairs write their totals in large numerals on self-stick notes and place their self-stick notes where all can see.

•• ••

•• ••

Mathematical Emphasis

Our place value system is based on an organizational system of grouping and regrouping.

Observe students as they count the beans, and informally assess their understanding of regrouping 10 sets of 10 to make 100.

Observe pairs working and, when appropriate, ask questions, such as:

Q. How many beans have you counted? How many groups of 10? Were there any left over?

Q. How many beans would you have if you added [four] more groups of ten beans? How do you know?

•• In pairs, students

1. Count the lima beans in their cups by 10s.

2. Use 3-oz. cups for grouping sets of 10 beans and 16-oz. margarine tubs for regrouping sets of 10 to 100.

3. Write their totals on self-stick notes.

4. Place their self-stick notes where all can see.

Notes	Teacher	Students

Notes

Encourage students to verbalize their thinking. As students explain and justify their thinking, check for understanding on the part of the whole class. Encourage students to address questions directly to each other.

Provide time after each question for students to solve the problem.

Students may need to use the beans to help them solve these problems.

Students will need to use a Two-Hundred Chart to help them explore these questions.

Teacher

With student direction, arrange the self-stick notes with the actual counts in order from lowest to highest. Ask questions, such as:

Q. What is the fewest number of beans? The greatest?

Q. Were the estimates reasonable? Why?

Facilitate a discussion about grouping and counting. Ask questions, such as:

Q. If you had [156] beans, how many sets of 100 could you make? How many 10s? Would there be any left over?

Q. If you had [2] groups of 100s, [4] groups of 10s and [3] left over, how many beans would you have? If you added [6] more groups of 10, how many beans would you have? How many beans would you have if you took away [4] 10s from 243 beans? How do you know?

Point to two self-stick notes with actual counts and ask questions, such as:

Q. Which one is closer to 100? How do you know? Are these numbers closer to 150 or closer to 200? Why?

Students

•• ••

•• ••

Notes

You might wish to write a frame sentence as a model for students to use if they choose. For example:

Our cup holds _____ lima beans.

Teacher

Give each student a sheet of paper. Have them title it "Lima Beans 1," write a sentence about the actual number of lima beans in their 8-oz. cup, and put the paper in their folder. Encourage pairs to help each other write their statements. State that they will use the statements during the last lesson of the unit.

Students

••

In pairs, students help each other write a sentence about the number of lima beans in their cup.

Notes

Teacher	**Students**

Teacher

Help students reflect on their group work by asking questions, such as:

Q. **What worked well for you and your partner today?**

Q. **How did you share the work? How did that work? What might you do differently next time?**

Q. **How did you act responsibly today? How did that affect your work?**

Students

•• ••

•• ••

Social Emphasis

Analyze the effect of behavior on others and on the group work.

Extensions

For Pairs That Finish Early

- Ask: "How many lima beans did you have in your cup? How many groups of 10? If you grouped the beans by 5s, how many groups of five would you have? How could you check your estimate?" Have students investigate this problem.

For the Next Day

- Continue with the "Number of the Week" bulletin board activity described in the Overview, p. 60.

- Continue with the next lesson, "Lima Beans 2."

Lima Beans 2

Students compare different-size containers to the 8-oz. cup used in "Lima Beans 1" and predict whether they will hold more, fewer, or the same number of beans as the 8-oz. cup. Students then group and count the contents of each container by tens. This lesson may take more than one class period.

DAYS AHEAD
4

Mathematical Emphasis

In this lesson, students

- Make an estimate.
- Count by 100s, 10s, and 1s.
- Compare capacities.

Students add to their understanding that

- Measurement is approximate. Objects can be measured by making direct comparisons.
- Making a reasonable estimate requires gathering and using information.
- Operations can be carried out in a variety of ways.

Social Emphasis

In this lesson, students

- Share the work.
- Use materials responsibly.

Students continue to

- Develop appropriate group skills.
- Relate the values of fairness, caring, and responsibility to behavior.

Group Size: 2

Teacher Materials

- 8-oz. clear plastic cup filled with large lima beans
- Empty container with a capacity other than 8 oz.

Student Materials

Each pair needs

- 8-oz. plastic cup
- 4 containers of different capacities (see Before the Lesson)
- Baggie with about 300 lima beans (see Before the Lesson)
- Twenty to thirty 3-oz. paper cups (from Lesson 5)
- Two or three 16-oz. margarine tubs (from Lesson 5)
- Self-stick notes

Each student needs

- Folder (from Lesson 2)

Extension Materials

Each pair needs

- Access to a calculator

Before the Lesson

- Collect 4 containers of different capacities for each pair. One of the 4 containers should be an 8-oz. container that is a different shape from the 8-oz. plastic cup. You may wish to ask students to bring in different-size containers.

- Fill a baggie with approximately 300 large lima beans for each pair.

Notes	Teacher	Students

Notes

Students will need their folders with their record of the number of lima beans that filled their 8-oz. cup from "Lima Beans 1" (Lesson 5).

A cooperative structure such as "Turn to Your Partner" (see p. xii) provides opportunities for all students to be involved in the discussion.

You may wish to write the words for the labels where all can see.

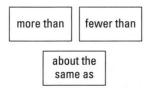

more than	fewer than

about the same as

Some pairs may label all their containers as holding more than (or fewer than or the same as) the 8-oz. cup.

Teacher

Introduce the lesson by asking students to discuss what they did in the previous lesson, "Lima Beans 1." Ask questions, such as:

Q. How many lima beans did your 8-oz. cup hold?

Q. How did you group and count the lima beans?

Show students an 8-oz. cup filled with lima beans and an empty container that has a different capacity than the 8-oz. cup. First in pairs, then as a class, discuss questions, such as:

Q. Do you think the empty container will hold more, fewer, or about the same number of beans as the 8-oz. cup? Explain.

Explain that pairs will predict if their four containers hold more than, fewer than, or about the same number of beans as the 8-oz. cup. Have pairs use self-stick notes to label the containers. For example, if a pair predicts that a container holds fewer beans than the 8-oz. cup, the pair will write "Fewer Than" on a self-stick note and attach it to the container.

Explain that after pairs label their containers, they are to fill the containers with beans and group and count the beans by 10s to determine whether their predictions were reasonable.

Students

•• ••

•• ••

Notes	Teacher	Students

As you observe, ask yourself questions, such as:

Q. Do students automatically assume that if a container is taller than the others it will have a greater capacity? (Students will construct an understanding of capacity over time. Provide students with many experiences comparing capacities.)

Q. Are students' predictions reasonable?

Q. Do students regroup 10 tens to 100, or ignore the regrouping process?

Observe pairs working and, when appropriate, ask questions, such as:

Q. Why do you think this container holds [fewer] beans than the 8-oz. cup?

Q. How are you sharing the work?

Q. How many beans fill this container? How many 100s? 10s? Are there any left over?

Q. What do you like about how you and your partner are working?

●● In pairs, students

1. Predict whether containers hold more, fewer, or the same number of beans as the cup, and label them.

2. Determine whether their predictions were reasonable by filling the containers with beans, then grouping and counting the beans by 10s.

Mathematical Emphasis

Measurement is approximate. Objects can be measured by making direct comparisons.

Provide sufficient time for students to explore these questions.

Students may choose to use calculators, paper and pencil, mental computation, or a combination of strategies to explore these questions.

Encourage students to verbalize or demonstrate their thinking. As students explain and justify their thinking, check for agreement on the part of the class.

First in pairs, and then as a class, discuss questions, such as:

Q. What did you discover about the containers?

Q. How do the containers compare with each other?

Q. Were you surprised by any of the results? Why?

Q. Which container holds closest to 200 beans? How do you know?

Q. Order your containers from the one that holds the fewest beans to the one that holds the most beans. What do you notice?

Q. What is the difference between the number of beans each container holds? What strategy did you use to determine this?

Q. How is this lesson similar to or different from the previous lessons?

●● ●●

●● ●●

Notes	**Teacher**	**Students**

You might wish to write a frame sentence as a model for students to use if they choose. For example:

The _____ container holds ____ beans.

Students might write, "The <u>tall, skinny</u> container holds <u>125</u> beans."

Hand out a piece of paper to each student. Ask them to title it "Lima Beans 2," write a sentence about the number of beans in each container, and put the paper in their folder. Encourage pairs to help each other write their statements. State that students will use the statements during the last lesson of the unit.

••

In pairs, students help each other write sentences about the number of beans in each container.

Social Emphasis
Relate the values of fairness, caring, and responsibility to behavior.

Help students reflect on their work together by asking questions, such as:

Q. How did you use the materials? Was that being responsible? Why?

Q. How did you share the work? Was that fair? Why?

Q. What might yo do the same or differently the next time your work together? Why?

•• ••

•• ••

Extensions

For Pairs That Finish Early

■ Have pairs determine the total number of beans all four of their containers hold. Pairs may choose to use a calculator, paper and pencil, or mental computation. Have them discuss why they chose that method and how well they think it worked.

For the Next Day

■ Continue with the "Number of the Week" bulletin board activity described in the Overview, p. 60.

Paper Airplanes 1

Students make paper airplanes, go outside to fly two trial flights, and cut a string the length of the distance of each flight. Students make chains of plastic links the length of the strings. They then group and count the links by tens to determine the distance of each flight, and record and compare distances. This lesson may take more than one class period.

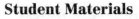

DAYS AHEAD

4

Student Materials

Each pair needs

- About 200 plastic chain links
- Paper
- String
- Scissors
- Paper clip

Extension Materials

Each student needs

- Crayons or markers

Mathematical Emphasis

In this lesson, students

- Measure distances.
- Group and count by 10s and 100s.

Students add to their understanding that

- Measurement is approximate. Objects can be measured by making direct comparisons.
- Numbers can be composed and decomposed.
- Our place value system is based on an organizational structure of grouping and regrouping.

Social Emphasis

In this lesson, students

- Help each other stay on task.
- Share the work.
- Find ways to handle disagreements.

Students continue to

- Develop appropriate group skills.
- Analyze why it is important to be fair, caring, and responsible.
- Take responsibility for learning and behavior.

Group Size: 2

■ Provide many opportunities for students to measure distance. Students need to explore, match, and make direct comparisons of distances. Emphasize the importance of placing units in a straight line and measuring using starting and ending points.

■ Find an appropriate area for flying the airplanes.

Notes	Teacher	Students

Introduce the lesson by asking questions, such as:

•• ••

•• ••

Q. Have you ever made a paper airplane? How did you make the airplane? (Have several students demonstrate how they make a paper airplane.)

Q. If we start here (point to a place in the room), **how far do you think a paper airplane can fly?**

Save the airplanes and record sheets for "Paper Airplanes 2."

Explain that pairs will make a paper airplane, fly two trial flights, measure the distance of each, and record each distance.

Social Emphasis
Analyze why it is important to be fair, caring, and responsible.

Ask pairs to discuss why it is important that they both agree on how to make the airplane. Have them suggest fair ways they might deal with disagreements.

Emphasize that each pair is to make only one airplane.

Suggest that pairs put a paper clip on the front of their airplane. The paper clip will help stabilize the airplane.

As pairs make their airplanes, ask questions, such as:

••

Q. How are you making decisions? Is that a fair way to make decisions? Why?

Q. Why did you decide to make your airplane like this?

In pairs, students agree on how to make a paper airplane, then make one.

Notes	Teacher	Students

Notes

Encourage pairs to develop their own methods of recording results.

Note students' social interaction as they fly their airplanes and ways they encourage and support each other.

If pairs' airplanes fly a distance of more than 200 links, have them mark the distance of 200 links on their string, then use the same links to measure the remaining distance.

Discuss how pairs might approximate measurements that are not whole links. For example, the length of a string may be 132 links plus part of another link. Pairs might approximate the length to be about 132 or 133 links long.

Teacher

Discuss how to conduct a "trial" flight. Demonstrate how to measure the distance of a trial flight by flying a plane and then cutting a piece of string the length of the flight. Remind students to keep their piece of string in a straight line as they measure the distance.

As a class, discuss ways students can help each other stay on task and why helping each other in this way might be important for this activity. Ask questions, such as:

Q. **What is meant by "helping each other stay on task"? Why might this help?**

Q. **What can you do to help you and your partner stay on task?**

Have pairs take their airplanes, scissors, and string outside and conduct the trials.

Bring pairs inside and explain that they will use plastic links to make chains the length of their strings. Explain that after pairs make each chain, they are to group the links by 10s and 100s, count them, and record the distance. Ask:

Q. **What could you do if you don't have enough links to make a chain the length of your string?**

Q. **What could you do if you can't make a chain exactly the length of the string?**

Students

•• ••
•• ••

••

In pairs, students fly their airplanes two times and cut strings the distance of each flight.

••

Notes	Teacher	Students

Observe pairs and ask questions, such as:

Q. **How far was your first trial flight? Was it longer or shorter than your second flight? How much longer or shorter?**

Q. **Did this string measure exactly [132] links? If not, what did you do?**

Q. **How are you helping each other?**

•• In pairs, students

1. Use plastic chain links to measure each string length.

2. Group and count the links by 10s and 100s.

3. Record the distance for each flight.

A cooperative structure such as "Turn to Your Partner" (see p. xii) can provide opportunities for all students to be involved in the discussion.

Ask pairs to report their distances for each of the trials, and list these distances where all can see. Ask questions, such as:

Q. **What is the shortest distance our airplanes flew? The longest?**

Q. **If we randomly picked one of our airplanes, how far might it fly? Why?**

•• ••

•• ••

Refer to one of the distances and ask questions, such as:

Q. **This airplane flew a distance of [179] links. If we grouped [179] links into chains of 10s, how many groups of 100s and 10s would we have? Would there be any left over?**

Provide sufficient time for students to explore these questions.

Students might choose to use the chains of 10 links to help them solve these problems.

Q. **If we grouped the [179] links into chains of 10 links, how many links of 10s would we have all together? Would there be any left over?** [For example, 179 = 17 sets of 10 with 9 left over.]

Q. **If the airplane flew [89] links fewer in distance, how far would it have flown? How do you know?**

First in pairs, and then as a class, discuss questions, such as:

Q. **What did you do that helped you and your partner?**

Q. **How did you help each other stay on task? How did that help you work?**

Notes	**Teacher**	**Students**

If appropriate, share some of your observations of the positive interaction and the problems you noted as pairs worked.

Collect students' airplanes and record sheets.

Explain that in the next lesson pairs will estimate the distance their airplane will fly on a third try.

•• ••

•• ••

 **Extensions**

For Pairs That Finish Early

- Have both students in the pair make and decorate paper airplanes that they can take home.

For the Next Day

- Continue with the next lesson, "Paper Airplanes 2."

Paper Airplanes 2

Students estimate the distance their paper airplane will fly a third time, make a third trial flight, measure the distance, graph the longest distance of their three trials, and analyze the data. This lesson may take more than one class period.

DAYS AHEAD
1

Mathematical Emphasis

In this lesson, students

- Make estimates.
- Measure distances.
- Group and count by 10s.

Students add to their understanding that

- Measurement is approximate. Objects can be measured by making direct comparisons.
- Questions about our world can be asked, and data about those questions can be collected, organized, and analyzed.
- Making a reasonable estimate requires gathering and using information.

Social Emphasis

In this lesson, students

- Help each other stay on task.
- Use materials responsibly.

Students continue to

- Develop appropriate group skills.
- Take responsibility for learning and behavior.

Group Size: 2

Teacher Materials

- "How Far Did Your Airplane Fly?" graph (see Before the Lesson)
- Markers

Student Materials

Each pair needs

- Airplane and record sheet (from Lesson 7)
- About 200 plastic chain links
- String
- Scissors

Each student needs

- Folder (from Lesson 2)

■ Make the following graph:

How Far Did Your Airplane Fly?

1-50	51-100	101-150	151-200	201-250	251-300	301-350	351-400	400 or more

Distances measured in plastic chain links

Notes

Mathematical Emphasis

Measurement is approximate. Objects can be measured by making direct comparisons.

Teacher

Have pairs discuss what they discovered in the first paper airplane experiment. Have them review their record sheet to see how far their airplanes flew in the first two trials. Ask pairs to estimate how far their airplanes will fly on a third try and record the estimates.

Explain that pairs will make a third trial flight and measure and record the distance (as they did for the previous trials). Review how to measure the distances of their third trials. Ask questions such as:

Q. **When you measure the length of string, what will you do if the length of string does not match the length of the plastic chain?** (For example, if it's between 133 and 134 units long.)

Students

●● ●●

●● ●●

Notes	Teacher	Students

Social Emphasis
Develop appropriate group skills.

Ask pairs what they learned in the previous lessons that will help them work well together. Ask questions, such as:

Q. What did you like about the way you and your partner worked together in the previous lessons?

Q. What might you do differently today? How will that help you work well together?

•• ••

•• ••

If pairs' airplanes fly a distance greater than 200 links, have students mark the distance of 200 links on the string, then use the same links to measure the remaining distance.

Have pairs complete their third trials and measure and record the distances.

•• In pairs, students

1. Estimate the distance, fly their airplanes, and measure the distance with string.

2. Use links to measure the length of string that represents the third flights' distances.

3. Group and count the links by 10s and record the distances.

Mathematical Emphasis
Making a reasonable estimate requires gathering and using information.

Ask pairs to report the distances their airplanes flew, and list their data where all can see. Ask questions, such as:

Q. How did you decide on your estimate of the distance your airplane would travel?

Q. Was your estimate reasonable? Why?

Q. Based on the distances the airplanes flew, about how far do you think one of the airplanes might fly if we flew it one more time?

•• ••

•• ••

Provide sufficient time for pairs to explore this question.

Q. What is the difference between the shortest and the longest distances your airplane traveled?

Notes	**Teacher**	**Students**
You may wish to do this activity in a second class period.	**O**n the class graph, have each pair plot the longest distance their plane flew in the three trials.	●● In pairs, students plot on a class graph the longest distances their airplanes flew in the three trials.

Notes	**Teacher**	**Students**
Mathematical Emphasis Questions about our world can be asked, and data about those questions can be collected, organized, and analyzed. **A**s an Extension For the Next Day, consider organizing the data using students' suggestions. For example, students might suggest that the data be organized on two separate graphs, one for the shortest distances and one for the longest distances.	**D**iscuss the graph by asking questions, such as: Q. **What does the information on the graph tell us?** Q. **If we repeat this activity in the next few months, do you think the results will be the same? Why?** Q. **What other data have you collected?** (The results of the other two trials.) **How might we organize all the data we've collected?**	●● ●● ●● ●●

Notes	**Teacher**	**Students**
You might wish to write a frame sentence as a model for students to use if they choose. For example: Our airplane flew a distance of _____ links.	**G**ive each student a sheet of paper. Have them title it "Paper Airplanes," write sentences about the distances their airplane flew in each of three trials, and put the paper in their folder. Remind students that they will use the statements during the last lesson of the unit.	●● In pairs, students help each other write sentences about the distances their airplanes flew.

Notes	Teacher	Students

Social Emphasis
Take responsibility for learning and behavior.

Help students reflect on their group work by discussing questions, such as:

Q. How did you help each other stay on task?

Q. In what ways were you responsible today?

•• ••

•• ••

Extensions

For Pairs That Finish Early

■ Have pairs experiment with folding the flaps of their airplane different ways to see if they can make their airplane go further, fly in circles, or stay in the air for a long time.

For the Next Day

■ Model writing several questions that can be answered from the data on the graph in "Paper Airplanes 2." Then, ask pairs to write questions that can be answered from the data on the graph in "Paper Airplanes 2." Ask pairs to choose one question to share with another pair, and have pairs answer each other's question.

■ Continue with the "Number of the Week" bulletin board activity described in the Overview, p. 60.

Where Does It Go?

Students sort the numbers they collected during the unit and reflect on their work together. This lesson may take more than one class period.

Transition Emphasis

In this lesson, students

- Sort numbers.
- Determine the relative magnitude of numbers.
- Reflect on how they worked together and thank each other.

Students add to their understanding that

- The relative magnitude of numbers can be described.
- Classifying and sorting requires the identification of specific attributes.
- Our place value system is based on an organizational structure of grouping and regrouping.

Social Emphasis

In this lesson, students

- Share the work.
- Explain their thinking.
- Listen to others.

Students continue to

- Develop appropriate group skills.
- Relate the values of fairness, caring, and responsibility to behavior.

Group Size: 2

Teacher Materials

- Transparency of "Where Does It Go?" group record sheet

Student Materials

Each pair needs

- Access to a Hundred Chart (see Unit 1, Lesson 8)
- Access to a Two-Hundred Chart (see Lesson 3)
- "Where Does It Go?" group record sheet

Each student needs

- Folder (from Lesson 2)

I think that 52 is closer to 50 than to 60 because 52 is only 2 more than 50.

Notes	Teacher	Students
	Introduce the lesson by facilitating a discussion about the mathematics that students have explored during this unit.	●● ●● ●● ●●
	Have pairs review the statements they wrote about the distance their airplane flew in the previous lesson, "Paper Airplanes 2." Ask students to report the distance of one of their trials, and write these where all can see. Help students compare the relative magnitude of numbers by asking questions, such as:	
Students may need to use a Two-Hundred Chart to help them solve these problems.	Q. (Point to one of the distances.) **Is [137] closer to 152 or 126? How do you know?**	
	Q. (Point to one of the distances.) **Is [174] closer to 200 or 155? How do you know?**	
	Q. **Which numbers are larger than 102, but smaller than 112?**	
	Ask pairs to review all the data they have collected in their folders and to discuss and list all the numbers.	●● In pairs, students discuss and list the numbers they have collected during the unit.
Students may place certain numbers in more than one box. The "Numbers that do not fit" box accommodates numbers that do not fit in any of the other boxes; for example, 110.	Show the "Where Does It Go?" transparency and discuss the directions. Model the activity by choosing a number from one pair's list, discussing with the class where to write the number, and then writing the number on the transparency. Discuss what to do if a number fits in more than one box and when a number fits in none of the boxes.	●● ●● ●● ●●

Notes	**Teacher**	**Students**

Social Emphasis
Relate the values of fairness, caring, and responsibility to behavior.

Facilitate a discussion about how pairs might work together. Ask questions, such as:

Q. Why is it important to listen to the ideas of your partner when working on an activity like this?

Q. Why is it important to give reasons for your ideas?

•• ••

•• ••

Students may need to use a Hundred Chart and a Two-Hundred Chart to help them sort the numbers.

As you observe students working, ask yourself questions, such as:

Q. How are students working together? What improvement has occurred in their ability to work together?

Q. Do students have a sense of the relative magnitude of numbers?

Q. What reasons do students give for putting a number in a certain box? Do their reasons make sense?

Observe pairs working and, when appropriate, ask questions, such as:

Q. How are you sharing the work? Is that fair? Why?

Q. Have you placed a number in the "Numbers that do not fit" box? Why?

Q. Have you placed any numbers in more than one box? Which numbers? Why?

••

In pairs, students sort the numbers they have explored during the unit into the boxes on the "Where Does It Go?" group record sheet.

Mathematical Emphasis

The relative magnitude of numbers can be described.

Show the "Where Does It Go?" transparency. Have several pairs share how they sorted their numbers. As pairs explain their thinking, encourage other students to ask questions and to state whether they agree or disagree and why. Ask questions, such as:

Q. Could that number fit in another box? Why?

Q. How did you and your partner decide which numbers to put in the "Numbers that do not fit" box?

Q. Is 201 closer to 400 or closer to 100? How do you know?

Help students reflect on their work together. Ask questions, such as:

Q. How is it different working with your partner now than it was at the beginning of the unit?

Q. What did you learn about working with a partner?

Give students time to thank each other for being partners and to say good-bye.

To help students develop their understanding of the relative magnitude of numbers and grouping and counting by 10s and 100s, have pairs investigate the activity in Extensions before going on to the next unit.

Extensions

For Pairs That Finish Early

■ Have pairs re-sort their numbers using boxes of their own choosing. For example, students might sort their numbers by those that are Closer to 75 or Closer to 125. Ask students to explain how they sorted their numbers and why their boxes make sense.

Where Does It Go?

Decide in which box to write the numbers you recorded during the unit. Some of the numbers can be written in more than one box.

Less than 50	**Closer to 50 than 60**

More than 50 but less than 100	**Closer to 90 than 100**

More than 150	**Numbers that do not fit**

Sorting and Informal Computation

Mathematical Development ████████

This unit builds on the concepts introduced in the previous two units. To foster students' understanding of operations and the relationships between operations, informal experiences with computation are emphasized, along with related experiences such as grouping and counting, and sorting and classifying. Students informally explore division and the relationship between multiplication and division as they estimate, graph, and analyze data. Students are also encouraged to formulate and test hypotheses and build theories as they explore and solve problems.

Social Development ████████

This unit focuses on helping students develop their ability to make group decisions. Students have many opportunities to make decisions and to reflect on this process. See Teaching Hints, p. 124, for questions you might ask throughout the unit to foster students' awareness of their decision making process.

This is the first unit in which students work mainly in groups of four. See Teaching Hints, p. 124, for a discussion about supporting students as they learn to work in groups of this size.

Mathematical Emphasis ████████

Conceptually, experiences in this unit help students construct their understanding that

- Operations can be carried out in a variety of ways.

- Operations are related to one another and are used to obtain numerical information.

- A known quantity can be compared to an unknown quantity in order to make a reasonable estimate.

- Quantities of objects and sets of data can be grouped and counted in a variety of ways.

- Numbers can be used to describe quantities.

- Classifying and sorting require the identification of specific attributes.

- Questions about our world can be asked, and data about those questions can be collected, organized, and analyzed.

Social Emphasis ████████

Socially, experiences in this unit help students to

- Develop appropriate group skills.

- Take responsibility for learning and behavior.

- Analyze the effect of behavior on others and on the group work.

- Relate the values of fairness, caring, and responsibility to behavior.

Lessons

This unit includes eight lessons and an ongoing sorting activity. The calendar icon indicates that some preparation is needed or that an experience is suggested for the students prior to that lesson.

1. Just the Facts, Please!
(page 127)

Team-building lesson in which students use informal computational strategies to find out information about themselves as a group.

2. Candy Kisses
(page 131)

Problem-solving lesson in which groups of four estimate, group objects, and divide informally.

3. Found a Peanut
(page 137)

Logical reasoning and computation lesson in which groups sort objects and divide informally.

4. Love Those Peanuts 1
(page 143)

Problem-solving lesson in which groups estimate, group, and count objects.

5. Love Those Peanuts 2
(page 147)

Problem-solving lesson in which pairs solve problems using their own strategies.

6. Love Those Peanuts 3
(page 151)

Problem-solving lesson in which groups divide a set of objects.

7. By Air, Land, and Sea
(page 157)

Logical reasoning and graphing lesson in which groups sort, collect, organize, and analyze data.

8. Our Poster Museum
(page 161)

Transition lesson in which students reflect on their experiences in the unit and have an opportunity to thank each other.

"Collection of the Week" Station

This ongoing activity is to be introduced after Lesson 3. Prior to Lesson 3, collect sets of objects that can be sorted, such as shells, keys, pictures of animals, costume jewelry, or rocks. Put each collection in a large baggie and place the baggies in an accessible area of the classroom. After Lesson 3, have students choose a baggie and sort the collection in several ways. At the end of each week, have a class discussion about ways students sorted the objects.

Materials

The materials needed for the unit are listed below. The first page of each lesson lists the materials specific to that lesson. Blackline masters for transparencies and group record sheets are included at the end of each lesson. Transparencies and other materials are available in the *Number Power* Package for Grade 2.

Throughout the unit, you will need access to an overhead projector, and students will need access to supplies such as counters, calculators, scissors, crayons, rulers, glue sticks, paper, and pencils. The calculators students use in this unit should have the constant feature and should all be the same type. (While it is important that calculators be available at all times, they are listed on the first page of the lessons for which they are particularly important.) If possible, each group should have a container with all of these supplies available to use at their discretion.

Please note that several lessons in this unit involve food. You may wish to use some other food or material to take into account any dietary restrictions or concerns.

Teacher Materials

- Baggies of objects for "Collection of the Week" station
- Materials for forming groups (Lesson 1)
- Baggie of candy kisses for each group (Lesson 2)
- *The Button Box* by Margarette S. Reid (New York: Dutton Children's Books, 1990) (Lesson 3)
- Baggie of peanuts (Lesson 3)
- Baggie with 10 unshelled peanuts (Lesson 4)
- Masking tape (Lesson 4)
- Transparency of "Love Those Peanuts 2" group record sheet (Lesson 5)
- Transparency of "Love Those Peanuts 3" group record sheet (Lesson 6)
- Large sheet of paper (Lesson 7)
- Lesson picture (Lesson 8)
- 24″ × 36″ sheet of poster board or paper for each group of four (Lesson 8)

Student Materials

Each group of four needs

- Access to ruler, tape measure, or other tool for measuring length (Lesson 1)
- Calculator (Lesson 1)
- Hundred Chart (Lesson 2)
- Counters (Lessons 2 and 6)
- Baggie of peanuts (Lessons 3, 4, and 6)
- "Love Those Peanuts 3" group record sheet (Lesson 6)

- Count by Tens Chart (Lesson 6)
- 15–20 small toy vehicles (Lesson 7)

Each pair needs

- "Love Those Peanuts 2" group record sheet (Lesson 5)
- Counters (Lesson 5)
- Calculator (Lesson 5)

Each student needs

- 8½″ × 11″ sheet of drawing paper (Lesson 8)

Extension Materials

- 4 candy kisses for each group of four (Lesson 2)
- Pan balance for each group of four (Lesson 2)
- Paper clips (Lesson 2)
- Large sheet of paper for graph (Lesson 6)

Each student needs

- Drawing paper (Lesson 7)
- 4¼″ × 5½″ sheet of drawing paper (Lesson 8)

Each pair needs

- Counters (Lesson 5)
- Calculator (Lesson 5)

Each group of four needs

- Construction paper (Lesson 1)
- Sets of buttons (Lesson 3)

Teaching Hints

- If this unit is the first time students have worked for an extended period in groups of four, you may wish to provide many opportunities for students to focus on their group interaction. Students might discuss how working in a group of four is different from working as a pair and what they learned working in pairs that might help them to work as a group. As students may need extra time to develop a sense of unity and identity as a group, you might also wish to include several team-building activities throughout the unit.

- As part of the process for developing group identity, the Extension For the Next Day at the end of Lesson 1 suggests that groups create names for themselves. If students have not had experience creating group names, you might wish to suggest a theme for the group names, such as a name that includes names of units of measure (for example, the Incredible Inches or the Mighty Meters), a name that reflects something they have in common (such as the Four 7s or the First Borns), or a group name made from parts of their individual names. Have groups develop a table sign with their group name to be displayed in their work area when they work as a group. Frequently refer to the groups using their group names.

- Some questions are suggested at the end of Lessons 2, 3, and 4 that may take students a considerable amount of time to explore. For example, in Lesson 4, after determining the number of peanuts in their baggies, students are asked "About how many peanuts would you have to add to your baggie to have 200 peanuts?" You will need to extend the length of these lessons or have students investigate these questions during other class periods.

- Have calculators available at all times during this unit for students to use when they choose. Throughout the unit, ask if any students have used calculators for their work and lead an informal discussion about their use.

- In lessons that require sorting, encourage students to sort in a variety of ways. Ask students what attributes they are using to sort. Point to an object and ask why students sorted it into that category. Ask if there are other ways the objects could be sorted.

  Note how students deal with objects that have overlapping attributes. For example, if students are sorting toy vehicles by the attributes "Goes in Water" and "Has an Engine," note where they place a boat with an engine, such as a tugboat. Point to an object with overlapping attributes and ask students why they sorted it as they did.

- Throughout the unit, observe how groups are making decisions and think about questions you might ask that will help students focus on how they make decisions, whether their process is fair, and how their process could be improved. Such questions might include:

  Q. **How are you making decisions? Is this working? If not, what else might you try?**

  Q. **How are you making sure everyone is agreeing to the decisions you are making?**

  Q. **What problems are you having making a decision? What might be a fair way to solve the problem?**

Assessment Techniques

Use the following informal assessment techniques throughout this unit and when indicated in a particular lesson. As you observe, note students' conceptual understanding, as well as their behavior (for example, some students may give up easily or exhibit a lack of confidence). Before a lesson, develop some open-ended questions or decide on an area to focus your observation. Accept students' responses, but also probe their thinking by asking follow-up questions that require them to explain further. Whenever possible, record students' responses.

The purpose of these informal assessment techniques is to help you determine students' understanding of sorting and informal computation. The purpose is not to determine mastery.

Students' understanding will vary from experience to experience, particularly as they are beginning to construct their understanding. Insights gained from these informal assessments will help you determine further experiences that students need.

Observe Individual Students Estimating, Grouping, and Counting

As students work, observe individuals and ask yourself the questions below.

> **Q. Does the student gather information or use a referent to make an estimate, or does the student simply guess? Is the estimate reasonable? Can the student explain why the estimate is reasonable?**

Some students may not be developmentally ready to use information or a referent when making an estimate. Do not force the issue. Rather, provide students with many opportunities to estimate. Students need many experiences estimating as they construct an understanding of the logic of using a referent to make a reasonable estimate.

> **Q. Does the student use a variety of strategies to solve computation problems?**

Observe how flexible a student is with numbers and operations. Notice whether the student uses the standard algorithm for all situations or, when adding 21 + 34 + 58, for example, decomposes the number and adds 20 + 30 + 50, then 1 + 4 + 8. Students need many experiences to explore a variety of strategies and many opportunities to discuss strategies and their appropriateness for different types of situations.

> **Q. Does the student identify and use one or more attributes to sort objects?**

Some students may identify the attribute of color and begin to sort a set of objects by color, but then switch to sorting by a different attribute. Some students may not be able to sort a given set of objects in more than one way. These students may be bound by their perceptions and will need many experiences sorting and classifying before they have constructed an understanding of sorting.

Student Writing

Throughout the unit, ask students to verbalize their thinking, and at times to explain their thinking in writing. During this unit, students write interview questions and explanations of how they divided a set of objects.

Just the Facts, Please!

Students develop interview questions, interview each other, and write number facts about their groups.

DAYS AHEAD
1

TEAM BUILDER

Team Builder Emphasis

In this lesson, students

- Write interview questions and record responses.
- Compute informally.
- Learn something about each other.
- Develop a sense of unity as a group.

Students add to their understanding that

- Questions about our world can be asked, and data about those questions can be collected, organized, and analyzed.
- Operations can be carried out in a variety of ways.

Social Emphasis

In this lesson, students

- Make decisions.
- Include everyone.

Students continue to

- Develop appropriate group skills.
- Take responsibility for learning and behavior.

Group Size: 4

Teacher Materials

- Materials for forming groups (see Before the Lesson)

Student Materials

Each group of four needs

- Access to a ruler, tape measure, or other tool for measuring length
- Access to a calculator

Extension Materials

Each group of four needs

- Construction paper
- Markers

Kyle and I have 13 pets all together. How many do you have?

■ Decide how you will form groups to work together during the unit. (See Forming Groups, page xiii, for random-grouping suggestions.) Prepare any materials needed.

Notes	Teacher	Students

Randomly assign students to groups of four. Explain that these groups will work together throughout this unit to sort objects; explore ways to add, subtract, multiply, and divide numbers; and continue to group and count objects.

Social Emphasis
Develop appropriate group skills.

As a class, discuss how working as a group of four might be different from working as a pair. Ask groups to discuss what they have learned about working as a pair that might help them in their group of four. Have several groups share their ideas, and list these where all can see.

Introduce the lesson by explaining that students will act as number detectives and interview each other to uncover number facts about their group and to get to know each other better.

As a class, brainstorm and list ideas of things that can be described numerically, such as ages, heights, number of people in students' families, number of pets students have, or hand length.

You will need to save this list of questions for Extensions For the Next Day.

Discuss what it means to interview someone. Have students suggest interview questions for the brainstormed topics, and write these questions where all can see (for example, "How old are you?" "How tall are you?" "How many pets do you have?"). Ask questions, such as:

Q. Does this question (point to a question) **make sense? If not, how could we reword it?**

Q. Which questions ask for the same information? What one question could we ask to get this information?

Model how to conduct an interview using some of the questions students suggested.

Notes	Teacher	Students
Students may need tools, such as rulers or measuring tapes, to help them answer some questions.	Explain that groups will choose three questions and divide into pairs. Partners will interview each other, and record the information. Then pairs will return to their groups of four and discuss the data they have collected. Model this activity with a group of students.	●● ●● ●● ●●
This unit emphasizes decision making. See the discussion about decision making in the Overview, p. 124.	**O**bserve students and ask questions, such as: **Q. How are you deciding on your questions? Does everyone feel included? If not, what might you try?** **Q. How are you recording the information you are collecting? How are you making sure the information is correct?**	●● In groups, students 1. Choose three interview questions. 2. Divide into pairs. 3. Interview each other and record the information. 4. Discuss the data they have collected with the other pair.
For example, a group might report that Keisha is 7 years old, Sean is 7, Michelle is 6, and Twee is 8. Have students find the total of their ages and discuss what fact the group might write; for example, "Our group's combined ages are 28." Write the statements where all can see.	**W**onder aloud about what "group facts" might be discovered. (Students might suggest such facts as their combined ages or heights.) Use the information that one or more groups collected and model how to find and write group facts.	●● ●● ●● ●●
Students may need to use calculators to help them determine the "group facts."	As groups work, ask questions, such as: **Q. What are some interesting facts you have discovered? What did you do to find this fact? How do you know this fact is accurate?** **Q. How do you know that is your group's combined age?** **Q. Is everyone participating? If not, what might you do to make sure everyone is participating?**	●● In groups, students use the information gathered during the interviews to discover facts about their groups.

Notes	Teacher	Students

Notes

A group might say, "We found out our combined ages are 28. Keisha and Sean are both 7, Michelle is 6, and Twee is 8. We know 7 and 7 is 14. Then we added 6 and 14 and got 20. Then we added 20 and 8 and got 28."

Teacher

Have groups share their facts with the class. Discuss questions, such as:

Q. **What information about your group did you find interesting? How did you put your facts together to find this information?**

First in groups, then as a class, discuss questions, such as:

Q. **One group discovered that their combined ages equal [27]. What are some possible ages of students in this group? Which ages make sense for students in the second grade? Would 8 + 8 + 8 + 3 make sense? Why?**

Q. **One group discovered they had 19 pets. How many pets could each student in this group have? Could some students have no pets? Could someone have 19 pets? Which seems to make more sense?**

Social Emphasis
Take responsibility for learning and behavior.

Help groups reflect on their interaction. Ask questions, such as:

Q. **How did you work so that everyone was included? If you had problems, how did you deal with them?**

Q. **What decisions did you need to make? How did you make these decisions? Do you think your method was a good one? Why?**

Extensions

For Groups That Finish Early

■ Have students create a name and a table sign for their group (see Teaching Hints, p. 124).

For the Next Day

■ Have groups create group names and table signs, if they haven't already done so. Have groups share their group names and reasons for choosing them.

■ Use the list of interview questions and generate some class facts, such as the combined length of all the hands in the class. These facts can be bound into a class book, "Little Known Facts About Our Class."

Lesson 2

Candy Kisses

Students estimate the number of candy kisses in a baggie, remove ten candy kisses to use as a referent, and, if they choose, revise their estimates. They then use their own methods to count the candy kisses and to divide them in a fair way. This lesson will take an extended period of time.

DAYS AHEAD
1

Mathematical Emphasis

In this lesson, students

- Make an estimate.
- Group and count.
- Divide informally.

Students add to their understanding that

- A known quantity can be compared with an unknown quantity in order to make a reasonable estimate.
- Quantities of objects and sets of data can be grouped and counted in a variety of ways.
- Operations can be carried out in a variety of ways.

Social Emphasis

In this lesson, students

- Make decisions.
- Include everyone.

Students continue to

- Develop appropriate group skills.
- Relate the values of fairness, caring, and responsibility to behavior.

Group Size: 4

Teacher Materials

- Baggie of candy kisses for each group (see Before the Lesson)

Student Materials

Each group of four needs

- Access to a Hundred Chart (see Unit 1, Lesson 8)
- Access to counters

Extension Materials

- 4 candy kisses for each group of four
- Pan balance for each group of four
- Paper clips

DAYS AHEAD
1

■ Prepare a baggie of candy kisses for each group. Put approximately 40–60 candy kisses (about 7 oz.) in each baggie.

Notes	Teacher	Students

Notes

You might wish to facilitate a discussion about the use of the candy kisses as a manipulative in this lesson and to explain that at the end of the lesson students will divide the candy kisses among their group to eat.

This is an informal opportunity for students to use a referent. Some students may not be ready to use a referent. Do not force the issue.

Teacher

Show a baggie of candy kisses and wonder aloud about how many candy kisses might be in the baggie.

Hand out a baggie of candy kisses to each group. Ask students to estimate individually how many candy kisses are in the baggie and to discuss the reasons for their estimates with their group. Have students report their estimates, and randomly list them where all can see.

Ask groups to take 10 candy kisses from their baggies and then compare this amount with the amount left in the baggie. Ask students to revise their estimates if they wish.

Students

:: ::
:: ::

Mathematical Emphasis

A known quantity can be compared with an unknown quantity in order to make a more reasonable estimate.

Observe groups and ask questions, such as:

Q. [Greta], are you revising your estimate? What information makes you think your new estimate is more reasonable?

Q. What is the lowest estimate in your group now? The highest? How do these compare with your first estimates?

:: In groups, students

1. Remove 10 candy kisses and compare this amount with the candy kisses left in their baggie.

2. Individually decide whether to revise their original estimates.

3. Discuss any revised estimates with the group.

Notes	Teacher	Students

For example:

Second Estimate

31–64   25–60

48–65   19–52

Students may need a Hundred Chart to help them compare the estimates.

Ask groups to report their lowest and highest estimates, and list these responses. Ask questions, such as:

Q. Why did you decide to change or not to change your estimate?

Q. What is the highest estimate? Lowest estimate? Is there a big difference between the lowest and highest estimates? Look at the estimates listed. Would an estimate of [43] be possible? Why?

Ask groups to decide on a way to find the number of candy kisses in the baggie, other than counting by ones, and then to count the candy kisses using this method.

Mathematical Emphasis

Quantities of objects and sets of data can be grouped and counted in a variety of ways.

As groups work, ask questions, such as:

Q. How are you grouping your candy kisses? How did you decide to use this method?

Q. Would you get the same number by grouping and counting in another way? Why?

Q. How are you including everyone in the work?

In groups, students

1. Agree on a method for counting the number of candy kisses in their baggie without counting by ones.

2. Use this method to count the candy kisses.

Actual Number of Kisses

48   42   38

45   44

Use a cooperative structure such as "Heads Together" (see p. xii) to involve all students in the discussion.

Ask groups to report the actual numbers of candy kisses in their baggies, and list the responses. As a class, identify the highest and lowest actual number of candy kisses and compare the actual number of candy kisses with the highest and lowest estimates. Have groups share how they grouped and counted the candy kisses by asking questions, such as:

Q. The ["Flying Numbers"] said they have five groups of [five] and [three] left over. How many candy kisses does this group have? How do you know?

Notes	Teacher	Students

Notes

Provide sufficient time for students to explore these questions.

Students may need to use their candy kisses to solve these problems.

Teacher

Q. The ["Silly Numbers"] have [34] candy kisses. They grouped them in groups of [10]. Did they have any left over? How do you know? How many groups of [10] did they have?

Q. [Serafina] says her group has [30] candy kisses. Does any group have almost [10] more than this group? How do you know?

Q. This group says they have [29] candy kisses. They have them in groups of [five]. How many groups of [five] do they have? Do they have any left over?

Ask groups to decide how to divide their candy kisses in a way that all agree is fair and then to divide their candy kisses.

Students

:: ::
:: ::

Notes

Some groups may agree on a method that does not give each person an equal share. Ask them to explain their reasons for making this decision and why they think it is fair.

Teacher

As groups work, ask questions, such as:

Q. How did you decide to divide the candy kisses? Why did you decide this was fair?

Q. How many will each of you get? Will you have any left over? What will you do with these?

Students

:: In groups, students

1. Decide how to divide the candy kisses in a fair way.

2. Divide the candy kisses.

Notes

Mathematical Emphasis
Operations can be carried out in a variety of ways.

Encourage many strategies for dividing, and emphasize the variety of strategies used. Compare and discuss the various strategies.

Teacher

As a class, discuss questions, such as:

Q. How did you divide your candy kisses? Did any group do it differently? Did you have any left over? What did you do with them?

Q. Everyone in [Henry's] group of [four] got [nine] candy kisses. [Three] were left over. How many candy kisses did his group have all together? How did you figure that out?

Students

:: ::
:: ::

Provide sufficient time for students to explore these questions.

Students may need to use counters or draw pictures to help them solve these problems.

Social Emphasis

Relate the values of fairness, caring, and responsibility to behavior.

Q. [Sira's] group of four has [41] candy kisses. They decided that they wanted everyone in their group to have an equal share. How many did each person get? If there were only three people in [Sira's] group, how many would each person get?

Q. If your group had 32 candy kisses and decided to share them equally, would you have any left over? How do you know?

Q. If everyone in [Marji's] group got 6½ candy kisses with one left over, how many candy kisses did this group have? How did you figure it out?

Q. What did you like about how you worked together? What problems did you have? How did you solve them?

Q. How did you include everyone? How was that a fair way to work?

To help students informally develop their understanding of computation, have groups investigate the activities in Extensions before going on to the next lesson.

**For Groups That
Finish Early**

■ Provide groups with additional, related problems to solve, such as:

1. If we put all the groups' candy kisses together, how many candy kisses do you think we would have? Why? (Students will need to be reminded how many candy kisses each group had.)

2. I used one bag of candy kisses for every two groups. Each bag cost $2.89. About how much money did I spend? (Students will need to be reminded how many candy kisses each group had.)

■ Ask students to write and/or draw pictures about how they divided their candy kisses.

**For the
Next Day**

■ Give each group 4 candy kisses. Ask groups to estimate how many paper clips it will take to balance the 4 candy kisses on the pan balance. Have groups record their estimates, and facilitate a discussion about the methods the groups used to estimate. Then give each group a pan balance and ask groups to find the number of paper clips it takes to balance the 4 candy kisses. Have groups report their estimates and discuss their findings.

Found a Peanut

Students suggest descriptive words, then sort and divide a set of peanuts.

DAYS AHEAD 3

Mathematical Emphasis

In this lesson, students

- Sort and classify.
- Divide informally.

Students add to their understanding that

- Classifying and sorting require the identification of specific attributes.
- Operations can be carried out in a variety of ways.
- Operations are related to each other and are used to obtain numerical information.

Social Emphasis

In this lesson, students

- Make decisions.
- Find ways to handle disagreements.

Students continue to

- Develop appropriate group skills.
- Analyze the effect of behavior on others and on the group work.

Group Size: 4

Teacher Materials

- *The Button Box* (see Before the Lesson)
- Baggie of peanuts (see Before the Lesson)

Student Materials

Each group of four needs

- Baggie of peanuts (see Before the Lesson)

Extension Materials

Each group of four needs

- Sets of assorted buttons (see Before the Lesson)

- Provide students with many experiences sorting objects.

- Play the attribute game Guess My Rule. For example, sort students according to a specific observable attribute that you do not name (such as collars/no collars on their shirts), and have them guess how you sorted them.

- If possible, read aloud *The Button Box* by Margarette S. Reid (New York: Dutton Children's Books, 1990) to provide students with another opportunity to think about and discuss sorting.

- For each group of four, prepare a baggie of about 20 unshelled peanuts. Prepare an extra baggie for demonstration purposes.

- For each group of four, collect an assortment of buttons and put them into a baggie for Extension For the Next Day.

Notes	Teacher	Students

Notes

Consider using an overhead projector to demonstrate how to

1. Sort the peanuts (for example, by the attributes cracked/not cracked).
2. Record the attributes used for sorting the peanuts.
3. Push the peanuts back into one group before re-sorting them by new attributes.

Teacher

Show a baggie of peanuts and wonder aloud about the different ways the peanuts could be described. As a class, discuss descriptive words, and list where all can see.

Discuss how these descriptions could be used to sort the peanuts. Explain that students will sort their peanuts in as many ways as they can, keeping a list of how they sorted them. Model sorting the peanuts and recording how they were sorted.

Facilitate a discussion about working as a group by asking questions, such as:

Q. **What are some ways your group has made decisions?**

Q. **What can you say if you disagree with someone in your group?**

Q. **What can you say if someone in your group disagrees with your idea for sorting the peanuts?**

Notes	**Teacher**	**Students**
Mathematical Emphasis Classifying and sorting require the identification of specific attributes.	Observe groups and ask questions, such as: Q. **How are you sorting your peanuts?** Q. **Why does this peanut** (point to a peanut) **fit here?** Q. **Do any of your peanuts fit in more than one group? If so, how are you handling this?** Q. **How else might you sort the peanuts?**	•• In groups, students 1. Sort the peanuts in many different ways. 2. List the attributes by which they sorted the peanuts.
	As a class, discuss how the groups sorted the peanuts. Have several groups model their methods with their peanuts. List the different ways the peanuts were sorted. Ask questions, such as: Q. **Did any group have a peanut (or peanuts) that belong to more than one category? How did your group solve that problem?** Ask students to decide on a way to divide the peanuts, other than giving them out one by one, so that each group member gets an equal share.	•• •• •• •• •• ••
Observe students and note the methods they use to divide and how they make decisions. Ask yourself questions, such as: Q. Do students include each other in making decisions? Q. How do students handle disagreements?	As students work, ask questions, such as: Q. **How are you dividing the peanuts? How do you know that each person has an equal share?** Q. **How many peanuts did you have? How many did each of you get?** Q. **Were there any left over? What did you do with them?**	•• In groups, students 1. Decide on a way to divide the peanuts. 2. Divide the peanuts so that each group member gets an equal share.

Notes	Teacher	Students

Notes

For example, a group may say "We had 22 peanuts and 4 people. We gave each person 2 peanuts. We had 14 left over. So we decided to give everybody 2 more peanuts. That left us with 6 peanuts. Then we gave everybody 1 more peanut. Each person got 5 peanuts. We have 2 left over."

Provide sufficient time for students to explore these questions.

Students may need to use their peanuts as counters to help them solve these problems.

Teacher

Facilitate a discussion about how the groups divided the peanuts by asking questions, such as:

Q. How did you divide your peanuts? Did any group do it differently? Did you have any left over? How did you deal with them?

Q. How many peanuts did your group have before you divided them? Into how many groups did you have to divide them? After dividing the peanuts, how many peanuts did each student get?

Q. Everyone in [Anh's] group got [5] peanuts and [3] were left over. How many peanuts does [Anh's] group have? How do you know?

Q. [Jacob's] group has [19] peanuts and [3] people. How many peanuts does each student have? Are there any left over? How do you know? If there were [4] people in [Jacob's] group, how many peanuts would each student have? How do you know?

Q. If a group of three students divides 21 peanuts equally, how many would be left over? How do you know?

Help groups reflect on their group work by asking questions, such as:

Q. Did you have any disagreements? How did this cause problems when you were working? How did you resolve them?

Q. What worked particularly well for your group today?

If appropriate, share some of your observations of how students made decisions you noted as groups worked.

140

For Groups That Finish Early

■ Begin the "Collection of the Week" activity described in the Overview, p. 122.

For the Next Day

■ Give each group a baggie of buttons to sort. Ask groups to

1. Sort and classify the buttons in many different ways.

2. List the ways they sorted the buttons.

3. Choose one of the ways, and sort the buttons by that attribute again.

4. Ask one group member to remain at the table with the sorted buttons. Have the other group members walk around to other tables and try to guess how other groups sorted their buttons. Have the student staying with the buttons answer other groups' questions about how the buttons are sorted.

Love Those Peanuts 1

Students estimate the number of peanuts in a baggie, view a baggie containing ten peanuts, revise their initial estimates if they wish, and count the peanuts.

Mathematical Emphasis

In this lesson, students

- Make an estimate.
- Group and count.
- Compare numbers.

Students add to their understanding that

- A known quantity can be compared to an unknown quantity to make a reasonable estimate.
- Quantities of objects and sets of data can be grouped and counted in a variety of ways.

Social Emphasis

In this lesson, students

- Make decisions.
- Include everyone.

Students continue to

- Develop appropriate group skills.
- Analyze the effect of behavior on others and on the group work.

Group Size: 4

Teacher Materials

- Baggie with 10 unshelled peanuts (see Before the Lesson)
- Masking tape

Student Materials

Each group of four needs

- Baggie of unshelled peanuts (see Before the Lesson)

This baggie contains 10 peanuts. About how many peanuts are in your baggie? With your group discuss your estimate of the number of peanuts in your baggie.

DAYS AHEAD 1

- For each group, fill one baggie with 80 to 120 unshelled peanuts. (Vary the number of peanuts in the baggies.) These baggies will also be used in the next lesson, "Love Those Peanuts 2."

- Fill a baggie with 10 unshelled peanuts to use to introduce the lesson.

Notes	Teacher	Students

Teacher

Introduce the lesson by holding up one of the students' baggies and wondering aloud about how many peanuts might be in the baggie.

Ask students to estimate individually the number of peanuts in their group's baggie and to discuss their estimates with each other.

Show your baggie to the class, and explain that it contains 10 peanuts. Ask students to revise their initial estimates, if they wish, and to discuss their revised estimates with each other. Have students report their estimates, and list these where all can see.

As a class, discuss questions such as:

Q. How many of you revised your estimates? Why? Did you estimate there to be more or less peanuts than in your first estimate? Why?

Q. What is the lowest estimate in the class? The highest?

Explain that groups will decide on a way to group and count their peanuts. Also explain that these baggies will be used in the next two lessons, and that at the end of the third lesson, students will be able to divide the peanuts and eat them.

Facilitate a discussion about working as a group and ask questions, such as:

Q. Why is it important that you agree on a way to group the peanuts?

Q. How can you make sure you are including each other in the decision?

Notes

For example:

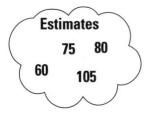
Estimates
75   80
60   105

Mathematical Emphasis
A known quantity can be compared to an unknown quantity to make a reasonable estimate.

Social Emphasis
Develop appropriate group skills.

Notes	Teacher	Students

Mathematical Emphasis

Quantities of objects and sets of data can be grouped and counted in a variety of ways.

Observe students and ask yourself questions, such as:

Q. Do students choose to group the objects or to count them by ones?

Q. Do students choose groupings by which they are able to count? For example, if students group by 3s, do they know the counting sequence 3, 6, 9, and so on?

Q. Do students include each other in the work? How?

Observe groups and ask questions, such as:

Q. **How are you grouping your peanuts?**

Q. **Would you get the same number by grouping and counting the peanuts in another way? Why?**

Q. **Do you have closer to [75] or to [125] peanuts? How do you know?**

•• In groups, students

1. Agree on a method for grouping and counting the peanuts.

2. Count the peanuts.

Keep the list of peanut totals for use in the next lesson, "Love Those Peanuts 2."

A cooperative structure such as "Heads Together" (see p. xii) can provide opportunities for all students to be involved in the discussion.

Students may need to use their peanuts as counters to help them solve these problems.

Ask groups to report their number of peanuts, and list these where all can see. Discuss the differences between the estimates and the actual numbers. Ask questions, such as:

Q. **What is the lowest and highest actual number of peanuts?**

Q. **Look at all of our estimates from the highest to the lowest. Are our estimates reasonable? Why?**

Q. **How did you count your peanuts? Did any group do it in a different way?**

Q. **[Sarah's] group decided to group their peanuts by [10s]. They have 8 groups of 10 and 5 left over. How many peanuts does [Sarah's] group have? How do you know?**

Q. **If you had 50 fewer peanuts, about how many would you have? 50 more?**

•• ••
•• ••

•• ••
•• ••

Provide sufficient time for students to explore these questions.

Q. If you removed 50 peanuts from your group's baggie, would you have more than 30 or fewer than 30 peanuts left in your baggie? How do you know?

Q. About how many peanuts would you need to add to your baggie to have 200 peanuts? How do you know?

Q. Your group had [110] peanuts. If my group had a little less than half the number of peanuts in your group's baggie, about how many peanuts might my group have? How do you know?

Q. How is this lesson like other lessons we have done?

Help groups reflect on their interaction by asking questions, such as:

Social Emphasis
Analyze the effect of behavior on others and on the group work.

Q. Did anyone feel left out of your group work today? How did your group handle this? How did it work?

Q. What did you find out about working together? How will this help you the next time you work together?

Give each group a piece of masking tape. Ask them to write their group name and the number of peanuts in their baggie on it and to stick the masking tape on their baggie. Collect the baggies for the next lesson, "Love Those Peanuts 2."

Extensions

For Groups That Finish Early

■ Have groups use a different grouping to count their peanuts. Ask questions, such as:

Q. Will counting the same number of peanuts by 1s and then by 10s give you the same results? Why?

Q. What if you counted the peanuts by 4s and then by 7s? Will you get the same results? Why?

For the Next Day

■ Continue the "Collection of the Week" activity described in the Overview, p. 122.

■ Continue with the next lesson, "Love Those Peanuts 2."

Love Those Peanuts 2

Students solve problems using their baggie of peanuts.

Mathematical Emphasis

In this lesson, students

- Solve problems.
- Compute informally.

Students add to their understanding that

- Operations can be carried out in a variety of ways.

Social Emphasis

In this lesson, students

- Make decisions.
- Share the work.

Students continue to

- Develop appropriate group skills.
- Take responsibility for learning and behavior.

Group Size: 2

Teacher Materials

- List of peanut totals (from Lesson 4)
- Transparency of "Love Those Peanuts 2" group record sheet

Student Materials

Each pair needs

- "Love Those Peanuts 2" group record sheet
- Access to counters and calculators

Extension Materials

Each pair needs

- Access to counters and calculators

Notes	**Teacher**	**Students**

<table>
<tr>
<td valign="top">

Post the list of peanut totals from Lesson 4 where all can see.

</td>
<td valign="top">

Divide groups into pairs. Introduce the lesson by explaining that another teacher with about the same number of students wants to do the peanut lesson and needs some information to prepare for the lesson. The teacher wants to know three things:

1. About how many peanuts she will need.

2. How many big bags of peanuts she will need to buy if each big bag fills three baggies.

3. How much the peanuts will cost if each big bag costs $2.49.

Show the "Love Those Peanuts 2" transparency and discuss the directions and the questions. Have pairs solve problems on the "Love Those Peanuts 2" group record sheet.

</td>
<td valign="top">

•• ••

•• ••

</td>
</tr>
<tr>
<td valign="top">

Students may choose to use counters, calculators, calculators, drawings, or mental computation to solve these problems.

To help students focus on the problem and analyze their strategies, you may need to ask questions, such as:

Q. What are you trying to find out?

Q. Have you thought about using a calculator to help you solve some of the problems?

Q. Does your solution make sense?

(ASSESSMENT)

As you observe students, notice whether they are able to persevere and to try different strategies if one strategy does not seem to work.

</td>
<td valign="top">

Observe pairs and ask questions, such as:

Q. **How are you sharing the work?**

Q. **How are you solving this problem? Why does your method seem to be working?**

</td>
<td valign="top">

••

In pairs, students discuss and solve the problems on the "Love Those Peanuts 2" group record sheet.

</td>
</tr>
</table>

Notes	**Teacher**	**Students**

For example, a student may say, "If you had $5.76, you wouldn't have enough money. We knew we needed three big bags of peanuts. We knew $2.49 is close to $2.50. We added $2.50 three times, so we know they cost about $7.50."

As a class, discuss the problems on the group record sheet. Have several pairs demonstrate and explain their strategies and solutions. Encourage students to ask each other questions. Discuss questions, such as:

Q. How did you solve the [first] problem? Did any pairs solve it differently? How?

Q. If I had $5.76, would I have enough money to buy the peanuts for the class? How do you know?

Q. How is this lesson similar to other lessons in this unit?

Q. How did you work together? What worked well? What problems did you have?

To help students informally develop their understanding of computation, have pairs investigate the problem in Extensions For the Next Day before going on to the next lesson.

Extensions

For Pairs That Finish Early

■ Have pairs discuss and solve:

  Q. How many big bags would I have needed to buy if each big bag filled only 1½ baggies? How do you know?

For the Next Day

■ Have pairs discuss and solve the problem below. Encourage pairs to use methods and tools of their own choosing, such as calculators, counters, paper and pencil, or mental computation, and then have them discuss how well these worked for them.

  Three classes worked on the peanut lessons. Together they had fewer than 700 peanuts. Ms. Smith's class had a total of 227 peanuts and Mr. Takimoto's class had a total of 346 peanuts. How many peanuts might Ms. Gray's class have in their baggies? How do you know?

■ Continue with the next lesson, "Love Those Peanuts 3."

Love Those Peanuts 2

As a pair, discuss the following problems and show in writing or pictures how you solved them.

1. About how many peanuts will be in all the

students' baggies?

2. How many big bags of peanuts will the teacher

need to buy if each big bag fills three baggies?

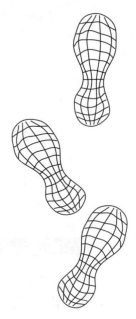

3. About how much will it cost to buy all the peanuts

if each big bag costs $2.49?

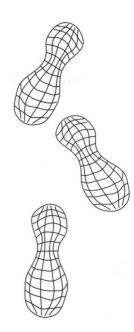

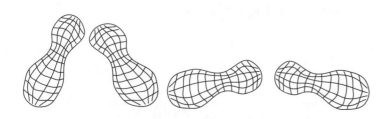

Love Those Peanuts 3

Students divide peanuts equally among their group members and write about how they divided them.

Mathematical Emphasis

In this lesson, students

- Compare numbers.
- Compute informally.
- Write about dividing the peanuts.

Students add to their understanding that

- Operations can be carried out in a variety of ways.
- Operations are related to one another and are used to obtain numerical information.

Social Emphasis

In this lesson, students

- Make decisions.
- Include everyone.

Students continue to

- Develop appropriate group skills.
- Take responsibility for learning and behavior.

Group Size: 4

Teacher Materials

- Transparency of "Love Those Peanuts 3" group record sheet

Student Materials

Each group of four needs

- Access to Count by Tens Chart (see blackline master)
- Baggie of peanuts (from Lesson 4)
- "Love Those Peanuts 3" group record sheet
- Access to counters

Extension Materials

- Large sheet of paper for graph
- Markers

We could each get 20 peanuts to start. That's 80 all together.

Then we could get two each until we divide them all.

I think we might have one left over.

Notes	Teacher	Students

Notes

A cooperative structure such as "Heads Together" (see p. xii) can provide opportunities for all students to be involved in the discussion.

Students may need to use a Count by Tens Chart to help them explore this question.

Teacher

Introduce the lesson by reviewing what groups did in "Love Those Peanuts 1" and "Love Those Peanuts 2" (Lessons 4 and 5). Ask questions, such as:

Q. **What was the total number of peanuts in all the baggies in our class?**

Q. **Is the number of peanuts in all our baggies closer to [700] or closer to [900]? Closer to zero or closer to [1000]? How do you know?**

Explain that groups are to decide on a way to divide the peanuts equally other than giving each student one peanut at a time. Encourage groups to try a method other than the ones they have used in previous lessons. Show the "Love Those Peanuts 3" transparency and explain that groups are to write or draw pictures on their group record sheet about how they divided their peanuts.

Students

In groups, students

1. Agree on how to divide the peanuts.

2. Divide the peanuts.

3. Write about or draw pictures showing how they divided the peanuts.

Mathematical Emphasis

Operations can be carried out in a variety of ways.

Observe students and ask yourself questions, such as:

Q. How are students sharing ideas and suggestions?
Q. Are students open to one another's ideas?
Q. Does any student tend to dominate the group discussion?

Observe groups and ask questions, such as:

Q. **Why did you choose to divide the peanuts this way? How many did each person get?**

Q. **What would happen if you divided your peanuts in a different way? Would each group member get the same number of peanuts? Would you always get the same number of peanuts? Why?**

Mathematical Emphasis

Operations are related to one another and are used to obtain numerical information.

Students may need to use counters to help them solve these problems.

Social Emphasis

Develop appropriate group skills.

Have groups share how they divided their peanuts. Ask questions, such as:

Q. How did you divide the peanuts? How many peanuts did each of you get?

Q. Everyone in this group of four has [21] peanuts and had [2] left over. How many peanuts does this group have all together? How did you figure that out?

Q. If there were twice as many peanuts in your baggie, how many peanuts would each person in your group have?

Q. How many would each person in your group have if there were half the number of peanuts in your baggie? How do you know?

Q. How is this lesson similar to others in the unit?

As a class, reflect on the group work by asking questions, such as:

Q. How did you work together? What worked well? What problems did you have?

Q. How is your group making decisions? What ways have you found that help your group make decisions?

Q. What ways have you found to disagree with others without hurting their feelings?

If appropriate, share some of your observations of the positive interaction and the problems you noted as groups worked.

For Groups That Finish Early

- Continue the "Collection of the Week" activity described in the Overview, p. 122.

For the Next Day

- Make and post the following graph:

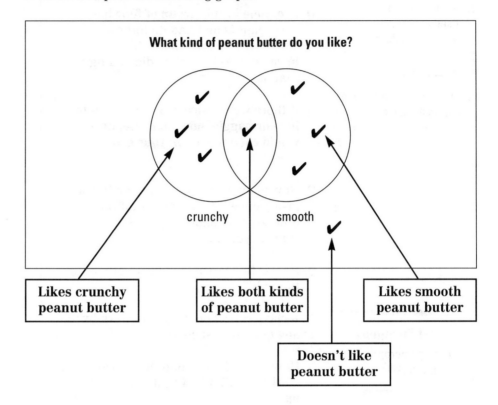

What kind of peanut butter do you like?

crunchy   smooth

Likes crunchy peanut butter

Likes both kinds of peanut butter

Likes smooth peanut butter

Doesn't like peanut butter

Ask students to talk with a neighbor about whether they like peanut butter and, if so, what type they prefer. Have several students share their preferences and, as a class, discuss where those students might mark the graph. Have all students mark the graph and discuss the results as a class.

Love Those Peanuts 3

In our group, we have _____ peanuts and _____ students.

This is how we divided our peanuts:

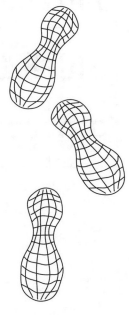

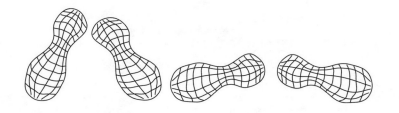

Count by Tens Chart

10	20	30	40	50	60	70	80	90	100
110	120	130	140	150	160	170	180	190	200
210	220	230	240	250	260	270	280	290	300
310	320	330	340	350	360	370	380	390	400
410	420	430	440	450	460	470	480	490	500
510	520	530	540	550	560	570	580	590	600
610	620	630	640	650	660	670	680	690	700
710	720	730	740	750	760	770	780	790	800
810	820	830	840	850	860	870	880	890	900
910	920	930	940	950	960	970	980	990	1000

By Air, Land, and Sea

Students sort and classify a set of toy vehicles to gather data to plot on a graph and then analyze the data. This lesson may take more than one class period.

DAYS AHEAD 3

Mathematical Emphasis

In this lesson, students

- Sort and classify toys.
- Collect and analyze data.

Students add to their understanding that

- Classifying and sorting require the identification of specific attributes.
- Questions about our world can be asked, and data about those questions can be collected, organized, and analyzed.

Social Emphasis

In this lesson, students

- Make decisions.
- Help each other stay on task.

Students continue to

- Develop appropriate group skills.
- Take responsibility for learning and behavior.

Group Size: 4

Teacher Materials

- Large sheet of paper
- Graphing question (see Before the Lesson)
- Markers

Student Materials

Each group of four needs

- 15–20 small toy vehicles (see Before the Lesson)

Extension Materials

Each student needs

- Drawing paper
- Crayons or markers

How many of our toy vehicles can go on land, in water, and in the air?

- If you do not have small toy vehicles, you might wish to borrow them from another classroom or ask students to bring them from home. If no toy vehicles are available, substitute another item that can be sorted.

- If students have not previously worked with toy vehicles, allow time for free exploration before this lesson.

- Play the attribute game Guess My Rule on the overhead projector. Sort some vehicles into two categories (for example, "wheels" and "no wheels"). Ask students what attribute you used to sort the toys, and list the categories. Push the toys back into one group and re-sort the toys using a different attribute.

- A graphing question is needed for the second segment of this lesson. You may want to create some possible graphing questions prior to the lesson; for example, "How many of our toy vehicles can go on land, in water, and in the air?" "How many of our toy vehicles have engines?" However, as you observe the groups' sorting, a more appropriate graphing question may become apparent.

Notes	Teacher	Students

As a class, discuss ways students sorted the peanuts in previous lessons. Show some toy vehicles and facilitate a discussion about how sorting the vehicles might be similar to and different from sorting peanuts. Explain that groups will sort the vehicles in as many ways as they can and record how they sorted the vehicles.

Social Emphasis
Develop appropriate group skills.

With a student, model sorting the vehicles and recording how they were sorted. Have students discuss responsible ways to work. If students do not mention the need to help each other stay on task, consider discussing the idea by asking questions, such as:

Q. **What has your group learned about working together?**

Q. **What can you do to help your group stay on task?**

| **Notes** | **Teacher** | **Students** |

Notes

Mathematical Emphasis

Classifying and sorting require the identification of specific attributes.

Observe the students as they sort the vehicles, and ask yourself questions, such as:

Q. Do students choose attributes that make sense?

Q. Do students identify and sort by attributes in a consistent way?

Q. Do students notice that some objects belong to more than one category? How do they deal with this?

You may want to do this segment of the lesson on the following day.

You may choose to use a bar graph, picture graph, real graph, Venn diagram, or some other appropriate graph. You might create the graph from students' suggestions. For example, a Venn diagram might look like this:

Does the vehicle have wheels and/or wings?

Has wheels   Has wings

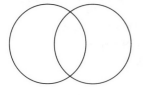

Teacher

Observe groups working and, when appropriate, ask questions, such as:

Q. What are your categories? How did you choose them?

Q. Why does this vehicle (point to a vehicle) **fit here?**

Q. How else could you sort the vehicles?

Q. Do any of your vehicles fit in more than one category? If so, how are you handling this?

Q. How are you helping the group with this activity?

Ask several groups to demonstrate how they sorted their vehicles. Encourage students to ask each other questions about their sorting methods. Discuss how groups dealt with vehicles that fit in more than one category.

Introduce and write a graphing question on a large sheet of paper (see Before the Lesson). Discuss the question with the class.

Students

•• In groups, students

1. Sort the vehicles in many different ways.

2. List the categories by which they sorted the vehicles.

•• ••
•• ••

Notes	**Teacher**	**Students**

You may wish to have an activity available to engage groups waiting to plot their data (see Extensions For Groups That Finish Early).

Ask groups to sort their toys according to the categories on the graph, count the number of toys they have in each category, and plot this data on the class graph.

•• In groups, students

1. Sort their vehicles based on the graphing question.

2. Count the number of vehicles they have in each category.

3. Plot this data on the class graph.

Facilitate a discussion about the data. Ask questions, such as:

•• ••
•• ••

Q. **What statements can you make about the data?**

Q. **How many more [airplanes] are there than [boats]? How do you know? Did anyone figure it out differently?**

Q. **Do more than half or less than half of the vehicles have [wheels]? How do you know?**

Q. **If there were 20 more airplanes, how many airplanes would there be?**

Social Emphasis
Take responsibility for learning and behavior.

Help the class reflect on the group work by asking questions, such as:

Q. **Did you need to help each other stay on task? If so, what did you do?**

Q. **What compliments would you give your group about how you worked?**

▶▶▶ **Extensions**

For Groups That Finish Early

■ Continue the "Collection of the Week" activity described in the Overview, p. 122.

For the Next Day

■ Ask individual students to design and draw a vehicle that can go on land, in water, and in the air. Have them write about their new vehicle, describing it and what it can do, and give it a name.

Our Poster Museum

Students review the mathematics they explored during the unit and reflect on what they have learned about working together. Each student draws a picture of the lesson they liked the most and contributes their drawing to a group poster. This lesson may take more than one class period.

Transition Emphasis

In this lesson, students

- Review the mathematical concepts they explored in the unit.
- Reflect on how they worked together.
- Thank each other and say good-bye.

Students add to their understanding that

- Numbers can be used to describe quantities.

Social Emphasis

In this lesson, students

- Share ideas.
- Listen to each other.
- Show appreciation to others.

Students continue to

- Develop appropriate group skills.

Group Size: 4

Teacher Materials

- Lesson picture (see Before the Lesson)
- 24″ × 36″ sheet of poster board or paper for each group of four

Student Materials

Each student needs

- 8½″ × 11″ sheet of drawing paper
- Markers or crayons

Each group of four needs

- Glue stick

Extension Materials

Each student needs

- 4¼″ × 5½″ sheet of drawing paper
- Crayons or markers

■ On the chalkboard, draw a picture showing something about a lesson in this unit. Below or next to the picture, write one or two sentences describing what the students did in that lesson.

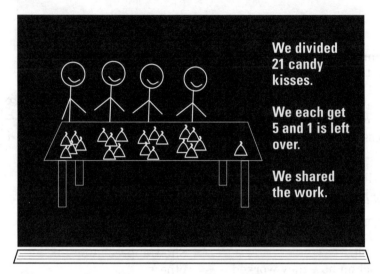

We divided 21 candy kisses.

We each get 5 and 1 is left over.

We shared the work.

Notes	Teacher	Students

Teacher

Introduce the lesson by explaining that groups will make a poster about the lessons they enjoyed in the unit. Review the lessons and ask students to think about the mathematics they explored and what they learned about working together. Ask questions, such as:

Q. Which lessons did you enjoy the most? Why?

Q. What mathematical ideas did you like exploring and learning? Did you like sorting? Finding different ways to solve problems? Studying the data on the graph?

Q. What helped your group work well together?

Q. How did you share ideas and the work?

Q. How did you include everyone?

As students offer ideas, list them where all can see.

Social Emphasis
Develop appropriate group skills.

Notes	Teacher	Students

Show your picture, read the sentences with the class, and discuss.

Explain that groups will discuss the lessons they enjoyed and decide on four pictures to draw. Explain that each student will draw one of the four pictures and write several sentences about the lesson and how their group worked together. Have students share their pictures with each other.

As students share ideas, reflect on how well they verbalize the mathematical concepts they have explored. Are they able to see connections between the lessons in the unit? Do they recognize that the "Candy Kisses" lesson was more than just eating chocolate?

Observe groups and, when appropriate, ask questions, such as:

Q. Why did your group choose these lessons? What did you like about these lessons?

Q. How are you helping each other?

Q. Were there any lessons you did not like? Why?

In groups, students

1. Discuss and decide on four of their favorite lessons and what pictures they might draw.

2. Individually draw a picture of a lesson and write about the lesson and how their group worked together.

3. Share their pictures with each other.

You may want to model different ways of arranging the pictures on the paper. For example:

Silly Numbers

Silly Numbers

Show students the sheet of poster board and explain that they will make a poster of their group's pictures by mounting the four pictures onto the poster, labeling the poster with their group name, having each student sign their poster, and hanging their poster in a designated area.

Notes	Teacher	Students

Encourage groups to explore different placements before gluing the pictures.

Observe groups and, when appropriate, ask questions, such as:

Q. How are you deciding where to glue your pictures?

•• In groups, students

1. Discuss and decide where to place the pictures.

2. Glue the pictures onto their poster board, label the poster with their group name, and sign the poster.

3. Hang their poster in a designated area.

You may want to do this part of the lesson in the next class period.

You may want to discuss briefly what a museum is and what things might be found in a museum.

Explain that the classroom has become a poster museum and that groups will take a "Museum Walk" to look at all the posters. Briefly discuss how students might stroll around the room without disturbing others. Ask students to walk around the room, viewing and discussing the groups' posters.

•• ••
•• ••

As you observe students, reflect on their ability to work in a group. Are they more comfortable with each other? Do they listen to each other? Are some students having problems working with each other? If so, which problems seem to be most evident?

As students view other groups' posters, ask questions, such as:

Q. What do you find interesting about this group's poster? How is it the same as your group's poster? How is it different?

••
••

In groups, students walk around the room, view the posters, and discuss them.

Notes	**Teacher**	**Students**

Ask students to return to their seats. Discuss questions, such as:

Q. Does any group have a question or want to say something about what they liked about another group's poster? Was there anything the same about the posters? Was there anything different?

Q. What did you like about the way your group worked together during this unit? Would you do anything differently next time?

If appropriate, share your observations of the differences between how groups worked together at the beginning of the unit and how they work together now.

Give groups an opportunity to thank each other and say good-bye.

Extensions

For Groups That Finish Early

- Distribute 4¼″ × 5½″ sheets of paper and have students draw a small picture of a lesson they liked. (A descriptive sentence is not necessary.) Have students glue their small pictures onto the poster they made during the lesson. For example:

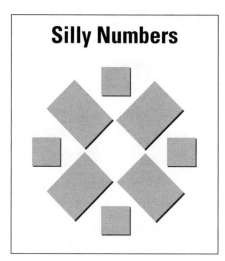

Additional Reading

Mathematics Education

California State Department of Education. *Mathematics Framework for California Public Schools, Kindergarten Through Grade Twelve.* Sacramento, CA: California State Department of Education, 1992.

———. *Mathematics Model Curriculum Guide, Kindergarten Through Grade Eight.* Sacramento, CA: California State Department of Education, 1987.

Ginsberg, Herbert P. *The Development of Mathematical Thinking.* New York: Academic Press, 1983.

Kamii, Constance. *Number in Preschool and Kindergarten.* Washington, DC: National Association for the Education of Young Children (NAEYC), 1982.

———. *Young Children Reinvent Arithmetic.* New York: Teachers College Press, 1985.

———. *Young Children Continue to Reinvent Arithmetic,* 2nd Grade. New York: Teachers College Press, 1989.

Kamii, Constance, and Barbara A. Lewis. "Research into Practice: Constructive Learning and Teaching." *Arithmetic Teacher,* 38 (1990), pp. 34–35.

Labinowicz, Ed. *The Piaget Primer.* Reading, MA: Addison-Wesley Publishing Company, 1980.

———. *Learning from Children: New Beginnings for Teaching Numerical Thinking.* Menlo Park, CA: Addison-Wesley Publishing Company, 1985.

Mathematical Sciences Education Board. *Counting on You: Actions Supporting Mathematics Teaching Standards.* Washington, DC: National Academy Press, 1991.

———. *On the Shoulders of Giants.* National Research Council, Washington, DC: National Academy Press, 1990.

National Council of Teachers of Mathematics. *Measurement in School Mathematics.* 1976 Yearbook. Reston, VA: National Council of Teachers of Mathematics, 1976.

———. *Developing Computational Skills.* 1978 Yearbook. Reston, VA: National Council of Teachers of Mathematics, 1978.

———. *Applications in School Mathematics.* 1979 Yearbook. Reston, VA: National Council of Teachers of Mathematics, 1979.

———. *Teaching Statistics and Probability.* 1981 Yearbook. Reston, VA: National Council of Teachers of Mathematics, 1981.

———. *Estimation and Mental Computation.* 1986 Yearbook. Reston, VA: National Council of Teachers of Mathematics, 1986.

———. *Learning and Teaching Geometry, K Through 12.* 1987 Yearbook. Reston, VA: National Council of Teachers of Mathematics, 1987.

———. *The Ideas of Algebra, K Through 12.* 1988 Yearbook. Reston, VA: National Council of Teachers of Mathematics, 1988.

———. *Arithmetic Teacher,* 36 (1989). Special focus issue on number sense.

———. *Curriculum and Evaluation Standards for School Mathematics.* Reston, VA: National Council of Teachers of Mathematics, 1989.

———. *Curriculum and Evaluation Standards for School Mathematics Addenda Series, Grades K Through 6.* Reston, VA: National Council of Teachers of Mathematics, 1991.

———. *Curriculum and Evaluation Standards for School Mathematics Addenda Series, Grades 5 Through 8.* Reston, VA: National Council of Teachers of Mathematics, 1991.

———. *New Directions for Elementary School Mathematics.* 1989 Yearbook. Reston, VA: National Council of Teachers of Mathematics, 1989.

———. *Professional Standards for Teaching Mathematics.* Reston, VA: National Council of Teachers of Mathematics, 1991.

National Research Council. *Everybody Counts: A Report to the Nation on the Future of Mathematics Education.* Washington, DC: National Academy Press, 1989.

————. *Reshaping School Mathematics: A Philosophy and Framework for Curriculum.* Washington, DC: National Academy Press, 1990.

Sowder, Judith T., and Bonnie P. Schappelle, eds. *Establishing Foundations for Research on Number Sense and Related Topics: Report of a Conference.* San Diego, CA: Center for Research in Mathematics and Science Education, 1989.

Stenmark, Jean K. (ed). *Mathematics Assessment: Myths, Models, Good Questions, and Practical Suggestions.* Reston, VA: National Council of Teachers of Mathematics, 1991.

————. *Assessment Alternatives in Mathematics: An Overview of Assessment Techniques That Promote Learning.* Berkeley, CA: Lawrence Hall of Science, University of California, 1989.

Cooperative Learning and Moral Development

Artzt, Alice F., and Claire M. Newman. *How to Use Cooperative Learning in the Mathematics Class.* Reston, VA: National Council of Teachers of Mathematics, 1990.

Brandt, Ron (ed). *Cooperative Learning.* Educational Leadership, 1989–90, 47.

Brubacher, Mark, Ryder Payne, and Kemp Rickett. *Perspectives on Small Group Learning, Theory, and Practice.* New York: Rubicon Publishing Inc., 1990.

Cohen, Elizabeth G. *Designing Groupwork: Strategies for the Heterogenous Classroom.* New York, NY: Teachers College Press, 1986.

Davidson, Neil, ed. *Cooperative Learning in Mathematics: A Handbook for Teachers.* Menlo Park, CA: Addison-Wesley Publishing Co., 1990.

Johnson, David. W., et al. *Circles of Learning: Cooperation in the Classroom.* Alexandria, VA: Association for Supervision and Curriculum Development, 1986.

Kohlberg, Lawrence. "Moral Stages and Moralization: The Cognitive Developmental Approach." In *Moral Development and Behavior,* T. Lickona, ed. New York: Holt, Rinehart and Winston, 1976.

————. *The Psychology of Moral Development.* New York: Harper and Row, 1984.

Kohn, Alfie. "The ABC's of Caring." *Teacher,* 1 (1990), 52–58.

————. "Teaching Children to Care." *Phi Delta Kappan,* 72 (1991), pp. 496–506.

Lickona, Thomas. *Raising Good Children.* New York: Bantam Books, 1983.

Reid, Jo-Anne, Peter Forrestal, and Jonathan Cook. *Small Group Learning in the Classroom.* Scarborough, West Australia: Chalkface Press, 1989.

Schmuck, Richard A., and Patricia A. Schmuck. *Group Processes in the Classroom.* Dubuque, IA: Wm. C. Brown, Company, 1983.

Schniedewind, Nancy. *Cooperative Learning, Cooperative Lives.* Dubuque, IA: Wm. C. Brown, Company, 1983.

Sharan, Shlomo. *Cooperative Learning, Theory, and Research.* New York: Praeger, 1990.

Teacher Resource Books

Baker, Ann, and Johnny Baker. *Mathematics in Process.* Portsmouth, NH: Heinemann Educational Books, Inc., 1990.

————. *Maths in the Mind.* Portsmouth, NH: Heinemann Educational Books, Inc., 1991.

Barata-Lorton, Mary. *Mathematics Their Way.* Menlo Park, CA: Addison-Wesley Publishing Company, 1976.

Barnett, Carne. *Teaching Kids Math.* Englewood Cliffs, NJ: Prentice Hall, Inc., 1982.

Burns, Marilyn. *About Teaching Mathematics, A K Through 8 Resource.* White Plains, NY: Cuisenaire Company of America, 1992.

————. *A Collection of Math Lessons from Grades 3 Through 6.* White Plains, NY: Cuisenaire Company of America, 1987.

———. *Math by All Means, Multiplication: Grade 3.* White Plains, NY: Cuisenaire Company of America, 1991.

Burns, Marilyn and Cathy McLaughlin. *A Collection of Math Lessons from Grades 6 Through 8.* White Plains, NY: Cuisenaire Company of America, 1990.

Burns, Marilyn, and Bonnie Tank. *A Collection of Math Lessons from Grades 1 Through 3.* White Plains, NY: Cuisenaire Company of America, 1988.

Collis, Mark, and Joan Dalton. *Becoming Responsible Learners: Strategies for Positive Classroom Management.* Portsmouth, NH: Heinemann Educational Books, Inc., 1990

Dalton, Joan. *Adventures in Thinking: Creative Thinking and Cooperative Talk in Small Groups.* South Melbourne, Australia: Thomas Nelson Australia, 1990.

Elementary Grades Task Force. *It's Elementary!* Sacramento, CA: California Department of Education, 1992.

EQUALS. *Get It Together: Math Problems for Groups, Grades 4 Through 12.* Berkeley, CA: Lawrence Hall of Science, University of California, 1989.

EQUALS, Alice Kaseberg, Nancy Kreinberg, and Diane Downie. *Use EQUALS to Promote the Participation of Women in Mathematics.* Berkeley, CA: Regents of the University of California, 1980.

Freeman, Marji. *Creative Graphing.* New Rochelle, NY: Cuisenaire Company of America, 1986.

Gibbs, Jeanne, and Andre Allen. *Tribes: A Process for Peer Involvement.* Santa Rosa, CA: Center Source Publications, 1987.

Graves, Ted, and Nan Graves. *A Part to Play: Tips, Techniques and Tools for Learning Cooperatively.* Victoria, Australia: Latitude Publications, 1990.

Hill, Susan, and Ted Hill. *The Collaborative Classroom.* Portsmouth, NH: Heinemann Educational Books, Inc., 1990.

Hosie, Barbara. *Maths About Me.* Melbourne, Australia: Longman Cheshire Pty Limited, 1991.

Kagan, Spencer. *Cooperative Learning.* San Juan Capistrano, CA: Resources of Teachers, 1992.

Lappan, Glenda, William Fitzgerald, Elizabeth Phillips, Janet Shroyer, and Mary Jean Winter. *Middle Grades Mathematics Project.* Menlo Park, CA: Addison-Wesley Publishing Company, 1986. A series of five books for grades 6 through 9.

Meyer, Carol and Tom Salee. *Make It Simpler: A Practical Guide to Problem Solving.* Menlo Park, CA: Addison-Wesley Publishing Company, 1983.

Morman, Chuck, and Dee Dishon. *Our Classroom: We Can Learn Together.* Portage, MI: The Institute for Personal Power, 1983.

Rhodes, Jacqueline, and Margaret E. McCabe. *The Nurturing Classroom.* Willits, CA: ITA Publications, 1988.

Richardson, Kathy. *Developing Number Concepts Using Unifix Cubes.* Menlo Park, CA: Addison-Wesley Publishing Company, 1984.

Russell, Susan Jo, Rebecca Corwin, and Susan Friel. *Used Numbers: Real Data in the Classroom.* Palo Alto, CA: Dale Seymour Publications, 1990. A series of six books for grades K through 6.

Stenmark, Jean, K., Virginia Thompson and Ruth Cossey. *Family Math.* Berkeley, CA: Lawrence Hall of Science, University of California, 1986.

Whitin, David J., Heidi Mills, and Timothy O'Keefe. *Living and Learning Mathematics.* Portsmouth, NH: Heinemann Educational Books, Inc., 1990.

Wilson, Jeni, and Peter Egeberg. *Co-operative Challenges and Student Investigations.* South Melbourne, Australia: Thomas Nelson Australia, 1990.